Love on Purpose

Ashley M. Coleman

Tamiqua,

Make your love

intentional

- Ashley

Published by WriteLaughDream, LLC. Copyright © 2015 Ashley M. Coleman

Cover Design by: Tiesha Miller

Author Photo: Shanina Dionna

ISBN: 0692811796

ISBN-13: 978-0692811795

Unless otherwise noted, Scripture quotations are taken from the King James Version of the Bible.

My love is intentional, deliberate, and on purpose.

CONTENTS

Chapter		
	Acknowledgments	i
	Introduction	11
One	Real Love is for Adults Only	17
Two	Definition of Love	21
Three	Decisions in Love	29
Four	Conquering Emotions	35
Five	Choosing Your Battles	43
Six	Communicating Effectively	51
Seven	Dying to the Flesh aka Killing Pride	59
Eight	The Company We Keep	65
Nine	Forgiving Quickly	73
Ten	Overcoming Fear	81
Eleven	Loving Yourself	87
Twelve	Building Trust	95
Thirteen	The Ability to Compromise	103
Fourteen	Unrealistic Expectations	109
Fifteen	True Intimacy	117
Sixteen	What Support Looks Like	125

Seventeen	Loving Enough to Let Go	131
Eighteen	What's In it for Me?	139
	Prayer	146
	Epilogue	147

God loves me. God loves me. God. Loves. Me. That revelation changes everything. Thank you God. And thank you to all those that he has placed in my life that love me and show me each and every day just how blessed I am. My husband, my parents, my closest girlfriends, and acquaintances. And to every single one of you that cares what I have to say, well, you give my life so much meaning.

Dear Children, let's not merely say that we love each other;
Let us show the truth by our actions.

1 John 3:18

INTRO

"Love is a decision, it's a choice." He said it so nonchalantly sitting across the table from me. I'm pretty sure we were eating or something, but don't hold me to that. My memory honestly sucks at times. As usual, I couldn't just take what he said at face value. I had to fight the notion at first. All this time I had learned that love was a feeling, an emotion, and that it was self-serving. Yet here was the man I was falling in love with, telling me something completely different.

After sitting with it for some time, I realized without a doubt that he was right. Think about it, "God so loved the world, he gave his only son." An action. He put this into motion because it was the way to give us life, the way to redeem us, the way He showed His love. He decided to save His people, He made a choice.

In dealing with family, forming friendships, meeting new people, and being in a relationship for over five years, I realized it was a disservice to myself to honestly reduce love to a feeling. Every single day, I realized I was making a choice. A choice to be there for my mom when she needs me, a choice to try to reach out to my family to spend time with them, a choice to encourage my significant other when he's down, even when I am trying to figure it all out for myself. The bottom line is, my walk in learning how to love people is filled with decisions. The moment we stop choosing, the moment we stop deciding to love, is the moment, most often, when we will find things falling apart.

When relationships crumble, it's because someone decided to stop trying. It's never one sided like we want to believe. "Oh this person did that" or "They did this to me and so ..." We make a decision, whether it's to be dishonest, to be unyielding, to be self-centered, whatever it is, we choose. We are all responsible for our actions, yet somehow in love we think some other force made us do it. Nope, it was just you!

It's funny because you never know where life will take you. It was love notes on Instagram that birthed my first book Dear Love. Well, it seems that not much has really changed because here I am again because of your encouragement, putting another book together. I felt that I couldn't just leave it at that. After a barrage of questions about "Dear Love Part II." I decided to do something just a little bit different. There was more to say and quite honestly you pushed me to say it!

But this is way more than just a part two. I really feel that Dear Love was the warm up to the meat and potatoes I hope to serve you with this go around. Dear Love introduced you to what may have been a new way of thinking about love for you and that's okay. So many of us have been caught up in the world's way of loving or the example or lack thereof our parents exhibited. But I am not afraid to tell you that God is your greatest example of how to love.

I know that may sound ethereal and spooky to some, but he loves us with an undying love. Agape love – meaning that it is unconditional, that there is nothing that can separate us from it, nothing we can do to screw it up and it will never end. As difficult as that is to digest in the real world, I most certainly believe that it is possible and the only way to actually make it through life unjaded by love. So many people move in the name of love with no idea what it really entails. This often tarnishes our perspective on love in the process.

In this book, I want to take a lot more of a practical look at love. Again, based on my experiences and what I have found to be true. I've never proclaimed to be an expert or anything of the sorts but I believe I have most certainly been given a revelation on love. It drives me, it breaks my heart when people are longing for it and can't seem to find it. So it's important to me to show you that whatever you want out of love, you have to be willing to put in. I did my time thinking that love was just supposed to work and wondered what was wrong with a person who didn't want to just love me for me. Let me tell you, it gets you nowhere quickly.

I want to be able to provide you with tangible ways to Love on Purpose. I want you to be able to actually put things into practice in your everyday life that will make you a more loving person. No matter the proper definition that you may find in the Webster dictionary; love is not just a feeling. It is not something that just randomly happens that we are entitled to play victim to. Love is not something that you can't choose or that just falls out of the sky. Love is an action word, it's something that you do and it has palpable ways of showing it. You do a disservice to yourself and the person on the receiving end of that love if you rest on the fact that love is a feeling. It's the easy way out to think that way. It's the way that allows us to run from relationship to relationship because we are constantly chasing a feeling with no foundation of what it really means to give or receive love. Not knowing that feelings can dissipate as quickly as they come.

As you read through this book, I also want you to open up

your mind up to the fact that it's not *always* about romantic love either. We should be loving people all around. It's easiest to love those that love us. But what about the people that are unkind? What about the people who have hurt us? What about loving people we don't even know?

Outside of love being something that we do, it's also something that should radiate from our being. We were created to love. It's the one thing that God said that would separate believers from the non-believers. We would be known by the way that we love.

The key thing to remember here is that love is not something that just happens to you. I've heard many people say you can't choose who you love, but I am here to tell you that you can choose how you love them. You don't have to be a victim to love. You can take control in any situation, at any time, you just have to make a decision.

It took me time to get there. I was willy nilly and floating on cloud nine just like so many other people. But as I began to actually work through love, stick with it, and be patient with it, I honestly began to see the labor of my hard work.

Don't be afraid that this isn't quite as poetic as Dear Love. I still intend to have a good time with you and give you a glimpse into my world as well. Let's have fun with love. Let's be honest about it. I pray that as you read through, your mind is alert and your heart receptive, because I think right here in this season, we have another opportunity to grow in love together.

It doesn't stop. I've learned so much about love over the last few years of my life. I have completely expanded my mind as to what love really takes. Sometimes I am on point and sometimes I am failing miserably and crying out to God like "Lord, I know better than this." We should continue to grow in love. Explore new facets, experience new emotions incorporated with it, and be enamored by its goodness. I am in constant motion with love and continuing to learn how to be better at it. Let's keep it going, let's cultivate an atmosphere of love. The world could surely use more of it.

Maya Angelou said this, "People will forget what you said, people will forget what you did, but people will never forget how you made them feel." Loving with every part of your being will give others an experience they may not ever get anywhere else. And I promise when loving after God's own heart, those on the receiving end will never forget how it made them feel. I am forever changed because I have known God's love and he continues to reveal it in new ways every single day. My prayer is that I learn to extend the same grace to people that he extends to me. And he extends it on the regular basis. Not because I am worthy, but because he loves me. We are made in His image, and so, we have the ability to save a life, heal, comfort and much more with the love that he has given us in our hearts to share.

Each chapter features a "Heart Check" with some questions to consider about each specific topic. Don't skip through them. Meditate on them, pray on them and give the most honest answers you can. Taking time to assess my heart has become an essential part of my routine. When I am in a disagreement with my significant other and think I'm right, sometimes I will be so convicted right away about whether my actions were of God or not. We can feel it. We know when we are being petty and when we are in the right. You have to be able to do that assessment yourself before you let your heart overtake your actions.

Most of what gets in our way in love is making permanent decisions based on temporary emotions. This is one of the worst things that you can do. Each Heart Check gives you that time you need to really evaluate a situation and be able to move on clearly and calmly to resolve it.

I am so ecstatic to be on this journey with you. I know that your life will never be the same when you experience God's unfailing love and begin applying it to how you love others. I know I have surely changed for the better.

It's my intent with this book to give you steps to take to love deliberately, intentionally, and on purpose.

REAL LOVE IS FOR ADULTS ONLY

I think this is one of the first things to get out of the way here. Real love is for adults only and the childish need not apply. Most often when there is constant conflict in love, there is one person who is a lot more mentally mature than the other. This can of course lead to detrimental issues that will plague the relationship, whatever they may be.

But it's something very important to note. As we go through the different chapters of this book, none of it will make sense if you are not mentally ready to make the shift from loving as a spiritually immature person to a spiritually mature person. So I think it best that if you are stuck in your ways, stubborn or the like that you close the book and pass it along to someone else who may actually get some use out of it.

I first heard this concept from my Pastor, Lester Brown of Authentic Life Church in Philadelphia and it literally blew my mind.

I thought to myself, "Wow, I have been extremely childish in my thoughts about love."

I always felt that the man in my life had to show me his love more so than I had to show my affection for him. And it sounds really silly when I write it out that way, but honestly that's what my actions showed. I was looking for him to always make me feel special and for him to make me feel wanted but I wasn't doing as good a job at returning the favor. Note to the ladies, men like to feel just as appreciated and loved as you do. Sometimes to varying degrees, but special nonetheless. I had to expand my mind to say, you know what, it can't be "me, me, me" all the time. That mentality was not going to get me where I wanted to be.

I've always believed that love is all there is. But my approach to loving has not always been the best. In my walk with Christ, I've learned that God is love. And there is no truer statement ever spoken. Loving others starts with God's love for us.

I am so glad to have found this type of love. But in the experience between two people you may not always *like* each other but you make important choices for the sake of love. Love is always being the bigger person no matter if you feel like that person was wrong or not. Love is immediate forgiveness. Love is sometimes doing the things that you really don't feel like doing. Love is delighting in doing something completely for another person that will not benefit you in any type of way. This is what I've learned about love and believe me, it takes a lot of maturity! It takes dying to our flesh daily.

Through ups and downs, hurt feelings, and whatever else comes with being in relationship with others, we have to learn how to handle it like adults. It's funny how quickly we can revert back to children, yelling, screaming, and throwing tantrums because someone hurt us or misunderstood something we did. Believe me, I have been there and literally thought to myself "There has to be a better way to handle this."

When I was a child, I thought as a child, (1 Corr. 13:11) but as I grow, as I mature, as I simply get older, I've had to change some of my ways. I had to learn not to take things so personal all the time. I had to learn how to resolve conflicts without completely losing my religion. I had to settle into being an "adult" in love and learning what that actually meant and how to actually showcase that to the people that I love.

We misconceive what it means to be in relationship with others. We think that certain things are "just the way that they are." But I have been committed to fighting what others may find acceptable. We don't have to yell and scream, we don't have to constantly be at each other's necks if that's not what we choose to do. We have the ability to make our relationships what we want them to be. We can indeed live in peace and be in love.

We run from "adulting" in various ways in our lives. I mean who wouldn't? When you get older, you realize just how great being a kid actually was. But we cannot take childish behavior into adult relationships and expect them to work out. Being an adult involves effective communication, maturity, letting down our walls, being vulnerable and getting rid of the "get you before you get me" mentality. If we are truly going to get all we can out of love, we simply have to grow up.

HeartCheck

Chapter One

- Do you find yourself having childish reactions in your relationships?

- Are you committed to the idea that love won't always be about you?

- How have you exhibited childish behavior in the past? What can you do to change it?

....

"If we are really going to get all we can out of love, we have to grow up."

DEFINITION OF LOVE

I thought that I knew what love was, as I have said before. And I had good examples of love. Not perfect examples because nothing is perfect of course, but I grew up seeing my parents' love and love from family and honestly watching love stories. I'm a sucker for a good love story, even until this day. It was great to have those examples, but it still wasn't enough. I had to get into it myself to see what love truly encompassed.

I always thought that love was about how it made me feel. The key in that sentence being "me." It's how we're set up to think about it from movies to music, to even sometimes our parents. But if both people in a relationship are constantly thinking about themselves, how will anyone be satisfied? It's kind of silly when you think about it right?

The reality is that if both people are constantly thinking about what will make the other person happy, both parties will always be fulfilled. In that way, relationships are investment opportunities. No, not in a way to make you money, but listen up. We are saying when we are in relationship with someone that we are invested in their well-being, their dreams, and their happiness. What we invest in our relationships will manifest a return. Your return is the fruit that is being produced. And the fruit will always be telling of the investment. If you are lazy, self-centered, and mean, what fruit do you think you will produce? We have to find ways to try to outdo one another in love and I promise you it will make for a very happy relationship if that is the focus of both participants.

So what is the definition of love? Well, let's first talk about the dictionary definition of love. According to Merriam-Webster, love is a feeling of strong or constant affection for another person. Attraction that includes sexual desire: strong affection felt by people who have a romantic relationship.

Do you see already how we are doomed to fail in the event that we take this definition of love at face value? First and foremost, do you see how they sneak in there "sexual desire?" Let me tell you that if you are basing the way you love on sexual desire, you are setting yourself up for failure. And that's just in a romantic relationship, but then how do you love others that you don't have a sexual desire for?

The next way this sets us up for failure is the word "feeling." That means that anytime you don't feel good about loving someone you can change your mind about it. Feelings and emotions are fleeting my friend. If you are talking about loving someone, anyone, a friend or foe, for an extended period of time, you cannot base loving them on how you feel. There will be highs, lows, mediums and more in loving someone. Yes, love makes you feel a lot of things but at the crux of it, love continues to be a decision in my book. But we'll get into that more in a little bit.

Lastly, this definition sounds great, but it gives you absolutely nothing in the way of how to maintain it, how to get through it or how to survive it. It just sounds good, but in my opinion it doesn't tell you at all what it means to love. Just to have affection for someone is not what will get you through the tough times, the misunderstandings, the miscommunications, hurt feelings, or the moments when you just want to throw in the towel. But I am so glad that I have a definition that actually helps with all that.

In the simplest form, my definition of love is God. God is love. When I first started writing those love letters on Instagram in 2013. I was writing those love letters to God. I was enveloped in a revelation of what it really meant that God loved me. I needed to know. I was having such a hard time forgiving myself for a lot of things. For my long-term relationship ending, for not believing in God before, for falling in love again, seemingly too soon. All those things were plaguing my spirit even though I thought I had dealt with them.

I want you to know a couple things. The first being that at our core, every single one of us wants to be loved. It is essential like food, clothing, and water to be loved. Some of us know love from an early age and some of us are seriously deprived of it and trying to navigate through this world with the damage that it has caused. Understanding that we all want to be loved is key. It was important for me to know that as special as I wanted to feel, I also had to help make the other person in my relationship feel that special. It is a cyclical notion to love another. Give it and get it. When we focus in on how the people in our lives want to be loved, we help fulfill an essential need in them. In turn, when they are fulfilled, they will also want to help fill that need in you. That shouldn't be your focus, but certainly an added byproduct to loving folks the way that they want to be loved.

I always heard about the book "The 5 Love Languages" by Gary D. Chapman, but I never really explored what it was about. It wasn't until a Life Group session with a group of women from my church that the book came highly recommended and I decide to read it. Changed my life!

The book breaks down that we receive love in 5 different ways – Gifts, Acts of Service, Touch, Words of Affirmation, and Quality

Time. I won't break them all down, get the book! But, essentially most of us give love the way that we want to receive it. But that doesn't mean that the person we're giving it to wants to receive love that way. We have to take the time to evaluate how people in our lives want to be loved. And better yet, ask them! After I read the book, I wanted to tell my significant other all about it. So we actually went online and did the test. Funny enough we actually have the same initial love language but found other things take precedent from time to time. We discussed it! We don't have to spend time guessing, because we actually communicated with one another about it.

Again, loving effectively, means putting another before yourself. Learning them and what really makes them fulfilled. And we all want to be fulfilled, so we're better people all around when we are. Meet the needs of another and your needs tend to be met as well. Of course there are exceptions to every rule, but you have to be willing to try to find out. At least then you know for sure that the relationship may be something you should move on from.

The second thing I want you to know is that knowing how much God loves you will help you immensely in your quest to love other people. Most often you hear that you have to love yourself first which I think is also important. But learning how God loves you will help you love yourself better as well as other people. The order is so important because it sets things up properly. If you are only ever thinking of yourself, that will always be your focus. If you are constantly putting others above yourself and God then others will always be your focus. Put God first and everything else falls in line. God thinks so highly of you, he adores you, and wow when you really let that sink in, you won't let anyone violate you, not even yourself.

There came a time when it clicked and I really got it. I finally felt like I knew that God was in my corner no matter what. It really came out of nowhere finally that God's love for me was not contingent on my behavior, but part of His being. Replace "Dear Love" with Dear God and you'll see. He loved me in spite of me and I learned that's how I needed to learn to love other people. I wasn't able to earn his love with my good works or getting an A on my Christian report card. I just had to truly accept it.

The greatest part about knowing how to define love through God's example is that he tells you exactly what things love exhibits and the things it does not. I will spare you putting the whole 1 Corinthians 13 verse in this book again, but I encourage you to look at it with new eyes. Two of the things that pop out the most to me about that scripture are two of the phrases that tell you what love actually does. Love believes the best and love never fails. They have taken me through a lot of the hard times I've had in love.

Love believes the best. I have to remind myself of this all the time. Sometimes the people that we love tap dance along the line of loved one and enemy. We can easily start to see folks we love as enemies with no real reason behind it. But I am here to tell you that we have to believe that person has our best interest at heart and that even in the times where they have hurt us, that it probably wasn't necessarily their intention. That doesn't count for people that we know are mean, malicious and angry. When you know that and there is no denying it, you have to remove those type of people from your life. But I am talking about when we know that the other person loves us and cares for us, but we treat them as if every mistake they have made or harsh word they have said was with the intent to destroy us. Why would you want to love someone like that? This phrase to me is just a constant reminder to believe in love and to believe in people and to trust that God will have your back no matter what. Sometimes I remind myself, "God is my protector." When I say this, I don't have to worry so much about constantly building walls to protect myself.

To put it even more plainly, sometimes I find myself in my own relationship thinking that my significant other made a decision that he knew was going to make me feel some type of way. Or that something he said innocently was meant with a sarcastic or malicious intent. There have been times when he has said "why would you think I would do that to you?" And I have to say to myself and him "I don't know." So many times I am projecting my own mean spirited will on the things that he does and it's not fair and it's unhealthy. Why is it that we want to be judged on our intentions, but we judge others solely on their actions? Sometimes, they simply didn't mean it in the way that it may have been received and we have to learn to forgive that quickly because we are all imperfect and in need of forgiveness at various times. When we can't believe the best in someone that we say we love, it may be time to re-evaluate that relationship.

And you know who else I had to learn to believe the best in? Myself. Not only did I have to rehearse this when it comes to the other people in my life, I had to rehearse it in my own mirror. It's interesting how the way we feel about ourselves can often affect the way that we feel about others. At times when I don't believe the best in others, I have found that I may be down on myself or untrusting of myself. Sometimes it takes checking our own motives as well to give us peace with how others are moving in our lives.

Love never fails. God's love will never, ever, end. Yes people change, seasons change and more, but God's love is completely unfailing. So for all those people who think they will never love again or are jaded about love, it will always come back around. I promise you. But you have to open up your heart and get some of that cynicism out in order to really see it. Knowing that love never fails gives us hope and in turn faith, because faith is the substance of things hoped for. Have faith in love, have faith in God and love will never fail you.

There have been moments in my life where I have been completely deflated, lost, and looking for direction. I've experienced things that I didn't understand and tragic losses in my life. But through it all, I know that God was with me, even before I was smart enough to realize it. He never failed. God never let me fall even when people, situations, and myself even, let me down. God's love was never ending.

You hear the term all the time, "looking for love in all the wrong places." Well I beg to differ. I think that we just look for the definition of love in all the wrong places and therefore our poor choices reflect that. Learn what real love is and real love is what you will attract. As long as we continue to entertain these falsehoods of love, we will never find it in the way that we want it.

We tend to let our friends, parents, television, film and everything else in the world define love for us and that's what most of us have been chasing after. All we will find is the world's love, which is fleeting, selfish and at the whim of how we feel at that very moment, that very day. That will not last. That will not stand the test of time. The love that has lasted lifetimes has been that of God, for His people and that is our greatest example and definition.

HeartCheck

Chapter Two

- ♦ Do you find yourself exhibiting some of the same behaviors that you saw in your parents' relationship in your own?

- ♦ What did you consider the definition of love to be before reading this Chapter?

- ♦ What has been most influential in defining how you think love should be? TV, film, friends?

....

"Knowing how God loves you will help you immensely in your quest to love others."

THREE

DECISIONS IN LOVE

"You can't help who you love." But you sure as heck can decide how to love them. Sometimes you have to decide to love someone from afar and you have to learn to be okay with that.

If we stick with God's example of love, then we can talk about the fact that God never stops loving you even if you don't believe in Him. But he lets you do your own thing and when you are ready to come back, he will restore you like the prodigal son. (Luke15:11-32). I believe it to be the same for us. Sometimes you have to love someone enough to let them go. Whether it's a friend, boyfriend, or close family member. We can't keep people around us that have constantly shown that they don't have our best interest at heart. It doesn't mean that you stop loving them. But we'll get more in depth about that in another chapter.

What I can't really flow with is when people act as if they have no rights or no decisions in who or how they love. It makes me angry because every day that I wake up I have to choose. I have to choose to be kind to a person that is being rude to me, I have to choose to be loving to my significant other even when I am not having a particularly good morning and the list goes on. All day I have to make the decision to walk in love. And sometimes I don't always succeed either. Some days I am impossible and some days it takes everything in me not to want to act outside of myself and like a fool. But I know that even in those moments, it's still a choice. It's so much easier to blame someone else or to act as if we have no control in a situation when clearly we do. Telling me that love is not a choice discredits every decision we make to walk in love when we could choose something else.

You are with someone who doesn't value you, you are friends with someone who is jealous of your life or you are constantly being berated by a co-worker. That is your decision to keep subjecting yourself to that behavior. You don't have to be nasty about it either when telling someone that you are no longer okay with accepting their choices because yes they are also choosing to treat you that way. You can be very kind in saying "I've decided that I love myself more than I love the way you are making me feel and so I choose me and I wish you well." Sure they should be better people, but the only person that you can control is you. So instead of frustrating yourself trying to make "adult" people behave, you have to learn to love yourself enough to make better choices.

Life is too short to be around people that don't want to celebrate you. I'm not saying that it's always an easy thing to do, but it is a necessary thing to do. Learn the value in yourself and you will make better decisions. If you think that love doesn't involve a decision what else in your life are you just letting happen to you?

Yes there is a good amount that happens in life that you cannot control. But you can control how you react to it. And you can decide to take a better hold of the things that you can control. Who you allow in your personal space and life is a decision. The reason that most of us run from that is because we don't want to believe that we have the biggest hand in the misery of our lives. I hate to be the one to break it to you, but we do. Your life is your own and some of the fruit that is being produced in your life is because of decisions that you make.

We are often our own worst enemies. But as I mentioned before, once we learn how highly God thinks of us, we begin to get a revelation of how highly we should think of ourselves. Never prideful or arrogant about our existence but knowing that we were put here for a reason and a purpose and we should be treated well, especially by someone that we say we love and that says they love us. When you get that A-ha moment, you will have no tolerance for being mistreated and you will find something different for your life.

Once you are in relationship with others, everything you do is a decision. Choose wisely in relationships. Think before you speak, remember to have others' best interest at heart, don't always treat people as if they have to earn your love, give it freely, the way God gives love to you. All these things are decisions.

I want to encourage you not only in love but in the rest of your life that you are in a lot more control than you think in a lot more situations than you think. The decisions that you make, will impact your life either positively or negatively. Stop thinking that you are a victim and take control of the things that you can. The victim mentality is so easy. Believe me I know. I spent some years of my life having that woe is me approach as well. It can't constantly be everyone else. We can't constantly shift the blame in our lives. You do not have to be miserable and mistreated in your relationships with others. It's not honorable or looked upon with merit. Choose to spend the most time with people that you enjoy and that enjoy you. Yes you will come across mean folks, love them anyway and try to get away from them as quickly as possible. But know that your happiness and well-being is ultimately your decision.

It's not always escaping a bad situation either. But you have to be able to recognize whether something is working for you or not. When I came to the end of an eight year relationship, I was faced with a decision. We had to figure out whether to keep living a hollow existence or to let each other go so that we could grow. He wasn't a monster, he was an amazing person, but the relationship stopped feeding both of us.

I could have just sat around and felt sorry for myself and been miserable that I was unfulfilled, but instead we decided to do something about it. And yes it was really, really hard and has taken me a lot of time to get over. But ultimately I feel we made the right decision.

Nothing worth having is easy. Every day of our lives we have to fight for our happiness in life. Our relationships are no different. Fight to either keep them going or fight to get out of them for your well-being. As in everything, it's a balance. You can't run at the slightest sign of tension, but I believe in the power of our intuition and you know when you know that it is time to let something go.

It's a scary place to be in to realize that you have the power to shape your life the way you want it. But I assure you that it will also be a liberating experience to guard your heart from being subjected to people who don't have a revelation of love in their hearts. Get yourself a piece of that freedom, give yourself that peace.

After you figure out whether a relationship or friendship is for you or not, the duration of the relationship will continue to involve decisions. Some simple ones and some extremely difficult ones.

Something quick that comes to mind is something as simple as deciding to do things that sometimes you don't want to do because you love another person. Being there with a friend through a break up, going to that sports game or concert with a girlfriend or boyfriend, when you couldn't be more disinterested. These are all sacrifices and decisions that make up the fabric of loving on purpose. If we are simply ruled by our emotions at all times, we would give our loved ones the most vicious side eyes any time they ask us to do something that we're disinterested in.

Often a decision I find myself having to make is choosing my battles as well. My best friend absolutely loves to debate. But somewhere along the way, I had to learn to stop even trying when I think she's wrong because the fact of the matter is even when she's wrong, she doesn't care. Ha!

But on a more serious note, you have to decide when to stand down, when to stand up for yourself, and when something is really just not even that serious. Life is really, really short, and if you are anything like me, you are uptight about a lot of things. The more I am learning to let go of the things that I can't control the happier I am! Everything in a relationship is not that deep. Plan accordingly. Know when something seriously needs to be addressed and when something might just be how that person is. Then decide whether you can accept that about them or not. You see where I am going here?

I don't want to bore you to death by using the word decide a million times, but I do just want to drive the point home. Like I said, each day, each interaction with another person will involve a decision. Will I be offended? Will I believe the best? Can I accept this or not? And sometimes one of the most important questions to ask is, "What am I adding to this situation?" "What can I do differently that may in turn affect their decision?" and "How might I be able to help resolve it? So often we are looking at another person through a magnifying glass and we never take the time to look inward and think of what we may be able to do to help a situation or something that we could have decided to do to help change an outcome. What will you decide to do to make your relationships better?

HeartCheck

Chapter Three

- Have you ever felt like you were powerless in love?

- What are some different decisions you could make to help improve your relationships?

- What questions may you need to ask yourself in regard to what you bring to the table?

....

"Learn the value in yourself and you will make better decisions."

FOUR
CONQUERING EMOTIONS

I know it may seem impossible to conquer our emotions. We are all emotional beings right? And yes I say all because women are not the only ones with emotions. Both men and women have emotions that they sometimes act on and in turn make some mistakes that they just can't take back.

Anger, resentment, fear, joy, anxiety, happiness, and more are just scratching the surface of the emotions that we face when we are in relationships with other people. Let's face it, at the moment we let people in, let our guard down and decide to say, "We love them," we are giving them a lot of power in our lives. We will in turn "feel" a lot of things as we go through the growing pains of loving someone.

But we have to begin to understand that emotions and feelings cannot be trusted. They are fickle and fleeting and if you base how you treat people on how you feel it is bound to be a roller coaster ride. Just think about it, from the time you wake up through the day, you probably experience a myriad of emotions. I don't know about you but I have gone from optimistic to anxious, to angry and everything in between. Imagine if I let every action be dictated by my emotions.

When I tell you this, it is from personal experience for sure. I am not short on emotions. I have a lot of them, I am passionate and I can be moody! But I had to learn very quickly in my relationship that high flaring tempers and emotions were going to lead us nowhere fast. I couldn't fly off the handle every time I didn't agree with something or when I felt offended by something that my significant other did.

How can you actually conquer your emotions? Well it starts with a little bit of patience. I had to learn for myself to just wait to speak. If I felt like we were having a disagreement, instead of letting it escalate, I would just walk away for a second or stop mid-sentence and wait a few minutes. Giving myself that brief pause helped me to be able to continue with the conversation without raising my voice or turning it into something a lot uglier than it had to be. I find that one of the basic requirements of being an adult should be having the maturity to disagree or bring up a gripe without trying to tear each other's heads off. It's possible. It's something that I am still working on too. It's all about breaking habits.

Initially many of us just react. We either ignore the red flags or they simply don't exist. That only leads down one path which isn't healthy in the long term. We can leave a trail of hurt feelings and tarnished relationships in that process. In my own relationship, I can appreciate so much more when we avoid the confrontation. Being able to resolve conflict peacefully makes it a little easier to remember to take the necessary steps to be better in future instances. It's a reminder that you can indeed live harmoniously with another person for the rest of your life even when you disagree. Relationships are all about what we choose. If you want to have a relationship where you yell and scream at one another, then great. Keep heading down that path. But if you want to be respectful of one another, then we have to make some necessary changes.

The fact of the matter is that when we speak out of anger or resentment or passion, we will without a doubt say things that we really don't mean and no matter what you were told as a child, words really do and can hurt. They can't be taken back. What you say in a moment can sting for the duration of your relationship with that person. Yes, they may forgive you but some words cut too deep to ever really forget. With that being said, I have learned to take every precaution not to say things that I don't mean. That involves thinking critically before I speak and learning to be in control of my own emotions. It takes really slowing myself down and not simply reacting and putting all of my petty aside.

When you are at the whim of your emotions, your relationships will be volatile. You will be madly in love with someone one day and then when you are no longer in a good mood, you will have one foot in the door and one foot out. Real love, real relationships, whether with friends or a romantic involvement cannot withstand the harsh environment of emotional decisions.

Think about how many times your boss makes you angry or does something that you don't agree with. Do you yell and scream at them and call them names and bring up things they've done in the past? How is it that we can exercise that type of restraint with basically a stranger and not with someone who we claim to love? The fact that we can control our emotions in certain situations and not others is a testament to the fact that they can indeed be controlled.

Someone might think that controlling your emotions means suppressing them and I want to be certain that I don't give you that impression. It is without a shadow of a doubt okay to *feel* things. It makes us human to experience the highs and lows of being in relationship with one another. You have to allow yourself the space to be intimate with your emotions. What I am saying is to take that time to process them on your own before you bring someone else into the mix.

If you are feeling anxiety, worry, fear or hurt in your relationship, deal with it first. Figure out the root of the problem. Work on how to articulate exactly what you are feeling to your partner. Sometimes in that process you may even find that it's not something important enough to bring up. Or when you sit with it, you may decide that you absolutely have to bring it to their attention. When it's important, when it's valid, there is no time limit on it. You won't forget. You will just be ten times more equipped to bring it to that person's attention and actually have a chance at them understanding exactly how it made you feel.

When we react emotionally, we immediately cut the line of communication. Think about it. Aren't you ten times more receptive when someone approaches you kindly? Well it sounds old school, but treat people how you want to be treated. How would you feel if your significant other was constantly approaching you in their feelings? You would not be receptive. You would not actually hear what they're saying and you will immediately be on the defense instead of being an avid listener.

In times when I have been in a heated debate or argument, at the point where our volumes are raised, I can literally no longer hear the person. It's crazy how that works. And then the fight becomes more about what's happening in that moment, "You're yelling at me," or "you're calling me names," and the original conflict never gets resolved.

There are no perfect relationships. I don't care what you see on Instagram and Facebook. You will have misunderstandings and sometimes disagreements, but how you handle them really makes the difference between relationships that thrive and relationships that drain. It's essential to learn how to communicate effectively and calmly. Finding a person or a friend that is sensitive to your feelings is a gem. When we are in control of our emotions we have an opportunity to make our concerns and our fears a lot easier to digest for our partners. If both parties are open and willing to hear each other out without getting emotional about what the other is saying, that creates a healthy environment for communication. When a person feels that they can't talk to you, they will hide things and/or they will find someone else to talk to about you which can be very dangerous. Friends are great to bounce ideas off of, but at the end of the day there is nothing you shouldn't be able to bring directly to your partner or friend after you've thought it over, let the emotion pass and properly thought about how to articulate that feeling to them.

Don't let your emotions ruin a good thing. I have seen it happen on many occasions. And I have been the victim of being in my own feelings on more than one occasion myself. I'm also often very defensive with my loved ones which is just another emotion. Automatically I turn on "protect myself" mode and that creates a wall as well. I am telling you how important emotion is because I have been there! I promise. I am constantly working through them in order to change how I relate to people I love.

Setting out on the journey to learn how to conquer my emotions has been an immense help in my communication with not only my significant other but my friends, and in professional relationships as well. I love that saying "Don't make permanent decisions based on temporary emotions." That lends itself to many different aspects of our lives, especially love. Do you want to be with that person? Do you want that person in your life? If the answer is yes, we have to learn how to better navigate the emotions that come along with loving someone.

It's also important not to confuse rash emotions with love. I find that especially with young people they think that anger and rage is somehow communicating how much a person loves them. IT IS NOT. I am here to tell you that no one that really knows what love is will think that jealousy and controlling behavior and anger is showing their love. Again, remember who your example is when it comes to how we should love one another.

Relationships contain two living breathing elements, people. Our human nature will not healthily withstand dig after dig after dig. Sometimes we think, "This is just how we are," and that may be the case, but I truly believe that over time that will wear down. The novelty will wear off and you don't want to be years in still all over the place and moving as emotional beings. Love has the ability to conquer emotions if you allow it to truly work.

HeartCheck

Chapter Four

- Are you letting your emotions cause you to make rash decisions in your relationships?

- Have you had trouble articulating your feelings calmly?

- What are the triggers that will cause an emotional reaction for you? How can you avoid them?

....

"When you are at the whim of your emotions, your relationships will be volatile."

FIVE
CHOOSING YOUR BATTLES

I talk about choosing your battles a lot and I think it is because it's been one of the hardest lessons for me to learn. On my blog, I've talked about how much I just love to debate and how I feel like it's so important to tell everyone how I feel about everything. Really, it was the worst when I was younger. I mean you couldn't say anything without me having an opinion about it. But as I get older, I honestly realize that every fight, every battle is simply not worth the scars that it leaves.

In the past, I felt like I wasn't vocal enough in my relationships. There were things sometimes I was afraid to say because of how they might sound or not wanting to necessarily hurt someone's feelings. I was extremely vocal in all other areas of my life, but there was something about being in relationship with someone that made me apprehensive to really be able to express certain things that I was feeling. This was probably the fear of losing that person that would make me retract in that way. But true love is knowing that people will love you past your flaws. But that's a whole different lesson. Fast forward to now and I can't stop telling my significant other how I feel about everything under the sun. I went from one extreme to the next and currently I am trying to find a lot better of a balance.

Everything that you experience with another person is simply not the end of the world. That is what I continually come back to when I am thinking about the things that I want to say and the things that I probably should just forget about or work through on my own. For instance, sometimes we can project our insecurities on our partners or friends. We find fault in certain things they do and want to bring it up, but really we are fighting an insecurity within ourselves. So sometimes a man may feel like his woman is hanging out too much and he thinks she should be at home. So, he constantly fights her when she wants to hang out with friends. This is a battle he is picking with her, but really he had an ex-girlfriend who cheated while she was always out with "friends." Well, that is something that he needs to work through on his own without causing damage to the relationship because of his past. His insecurity is being projected onto his current relationship.

So many of us project those types of things on to our partners and we don't even realize it. And here we think it's something that they are doing, but really it's us. The seeds that have been planted in us bloom where they don't belong. We have to be able to identify those things as they can be cancerous to our relationships. How can we begin to treat each new relationship as its own? I know, impossible right? Though we cannot erase our pasts and the impact that it has on the people that we become, we have to be able to give each new person a chance. Be aware of the signs, sure. You may see patterns that you recognize and can guess where it leads. But that's up to you to be smart and utilize your wisdom there.

The other part of choosing your battles is the fact that sometimes people we love just do ridiculous things that piss us off. It's inevitable. But I always try to remember that I am not perfect either.

There are things that I have done to disappoint friends or times when I have hurt my significant other's feelings. But how would I feel if they took every opportunity to tell me about it? We all make mistakes. Every single one of us. Some are bigger than others and who doesn't want to be able to sweep some of the smaller ones under the rug? I know I do at times.

Invest the time into your partner to know what battles are important. You know when you have to push them to be better and you know when pushing them is just going to make them retreat. Be caring, be kind, and be loving. Be sensitive to the needs of your partner. And if you don't really know the ins and outs of your partner in that way, you should take the time to analyze them. How can you be in love if you don't even know how to fulfill your partner's needs? Know when to hold them and when to fold them.

The perfect example is the fact that my significant other teaches young people that can be for lack of a better phrase, trying. On days when he has had a really tough day with the kids, it would simply not be smart on my part to bring up the trash that he forgot to take out. And yes, there have been times when I have completely missed the mark with this type of thing. But as I grow and mature in what it means to really be in love as an adult, I have to be able to pack up my gripes at times and store them away and simply listen and be there for him.

I've also found that a lot of times my need for battle was based on my need for control. I want things for the most part to be my way all of the time. Often I think my way is the best way. But I am smart enough to know now that is such a silly way to think. I have to give my loved ones the room to be themselves and not pick with every decision that they make that is different from mine. Being a control freak was making me crazy! I never even thought of myself as super controlling, but I realize that I was and that it was the source of a lot of my anxiety and anger. We have to learn to love one another without the need to try to control. You may not want to admit it, but is the source of some of your strife trying to control another person? Be honest about that and try making that adjustment. Learning your partner is important, but learning yourself is even more so. You are the only one you control in all your relationships. You're the constant. That's something to take into account. Find the similarities in how you relate to others and I am sure that you will find some things you'll want to change that will make your relationships flow a bit better. It is not always the other person.

Another factor in learning how to choose my battles was realizing that everything just isn't that deep and some of the crazy things that my partner or friends may do has nothing to do with me. We take so many things personally and to heart and wonder why it feels like love is kicking our butt.

Love is not easily offended and love believes the best. When you put those two things into practice, things get easier. You can't be afraid if that process takes time. In the beginning of relationships we are often on our best behavior and so we're easily offended whenever things go awry. Well, maybe not you, but I was. I took everything so personal and "what do you mean by that?" in the beginning. But I realize now it was a product of just being so fresh in my relationship.

But again, you learn your partner, your friends, or your family after some time. If you are attentive enough, you will learn what things you should take to heart and when you should just flag them and go about your business. That flag has saved me from many opportunities to get upset or angry about something that simply didn't warrant that behavior.

You have an aunt that's overly critical or a friend that's blunt, understand that's just who they are. You do not have to internalize that. You get to say, "You know what? They're crazy," and move on. Is it right that they're that way? No not necessarily, but you are the only one that you can control. So are you going to spend your life battling with folks that are unlikely to change or are you going to live your life and be great, which will always end up attracting the right kind of people? I choose the latter for sure! And it doesn't mean that I have to love them any less. Maybe I have to love them in doses but that's okay too. I've learned that how people relate to you has everything to do with who they are and a tiny bit to do with who you are, most often.

Then there will be times when you know, what you know, what you know and you have to be able to stand up for yourself or speak up. Maybe your significant other is spending too much time with friends and not enough quality time with you. Or your parent is not as supportive of your career path as you really would like them to be. These are examples of things worth battling over. And it doesn't have to be a blood bath. As we talked about in the previous chapter, don't bring these things to their attention after you have been listening to Drake and you're completely in your feelings. You have to let it simmer, give it time and then approach the situation. Speak the truth in love and it will always be a lot better received that way.

I'll never forget talking to a friend of mine about relationships and she told me about her practice of the Art of Shut Up. After my initial laughter, I realized she was definitely on to something. The art of shut up, I learned in that conversation is essential in successful and peaceful relationships. That is the moment when you evaluate, is what I have to say worth ruining the rest of my night or do I just want to shut up for the time being and save this for a later date?

I've heard from many guy friends that it can often seem like all women do is criticize. No real surprise there right? I didn't think it was that deep, but after I took an account, I can definitely say that if I am not conscious of it, I can seem to point out a lot that my significant other does wrong. This is not to say that you will never have another gripe because let's face it, you certainly will. But we can find some key times to practice the art of shut up here. Most often after your significant other has had a long, trying day, it really may not be the right time to tell them that they forgot to return something of yours or they need to take you out more. Finding the right timing is so important! I haven't truly mastered this yet, but I am working on it.

Pretty much we just have to learn, both men and women about timing. Some people may be great at this already, but I know I wasn't. I also love to have the last word and can't really stand when people think they're right and they're clearly wrong. But I have had to learn that sometimes that last word or being right, really is not as important as it seems in the moment. You can argue something to the death and be right and have no one around in the end to care about it.

Just like everything in life, it's a balance. It's not about being seen and not heard or anything like that. But I assure you that you will see an immediate result when you simply learn how to choose your battles. The longer you are with a person, the more you realize certain things just don't cause for that type of energy. We also have to be able to determine whether we are just being faultfinders and complainers or if the things that are plaguing us really have merit. This may sound really morbid, but I sometimes think to myself, what if I lost him today? Would I care about the dishes left in the sink or the music being too loud? It may seem dramatic, but really. God forbid anything happened to our significant others, we would be begging for those small things to be present.

So this is why it's important to me and should be important to you to think about what REALLY matters. Yes we will still probably yell about shoes in the floor and things like that, we're human. But sometimes you will just need to be that listening ear and whatever you were mad about will have to wait. Or sometimes you have to allow a person to make their own mistakes instead of constantly trying to tell them what you know is right, which is extremely hard but can be necessary. Just like parenting. Do you know how hard it must have been for our parents to give us the room to make our own mistakes? I don't know about you, but I cringe at some of the things I thought were right at the time and realized my parents just allowed me that room to grow.

Ultimately like most things in relationships, the art of shut up takes, humility, vulnerability, and caring about someone else sometimes more than your own immediate needs at the moment. Not easy, but possible.

When we do finally have the opportunity to voice our concerns, will the person on the receiving end always be as receptive as you would like? NO! So that's the first thing to realize. You can't throw everything out the window once that person doesn't respond the way that you want them to. You have to just keep trying to drive home and communicate your feelings and see how it goes. And if they start getting defensive and yelling, you have to try your best to maintain your composure. Sounds superhuman right? Well we can't do it in our own strength. That is where God comes in, in my life. You have to be able to operate in the spirit because when operating in the flesh, you will probably reach across the table and choke the person that you're talking to. But in reality, you are capable of so much more.

At the end of it, when you have refined your approach to disagreements and misunderstandings, you will know that you have done all you can do. In the event that person is stubborn and selfish and doesn't want to hear you out, well, that's on them. We are only accountable for our own actions in this life and the next. And sometimes the best way for someone to learn is to lose something that meant a lot to them. Unfortunately, there are times where relationships do end. Times when people just can't seem to get past the difficulties. But think of the peace that you can have when you say, "I did my best." When we do our best, God is pleased, and he will continue to bring people in your life that get it and that get you. Don't be afraid to cut the fat, in love of course!

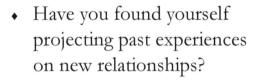

Chapter Five

- Have you found yourself projecting past experiences on new relationships?

- How might you be able to choose better timing for conflict resolution?

- Are you having serious gripes in your relationship or are you being a fault finder?

....

"Love is not easily offended and love believes the best."

COMMUNICATING EFFECTIVELY

We have partially addressed communication in the previous chapter. That was one part of communication, knowing when to communicate. But it goes a lot deeper for sure. Everyone talks about how important communication is, yet and still, so many of us completely suck at it. Myself included at times, but I am learning just how important it is when it comes to loving others.

Part of my biggest problem with communicating, I feel is an issue for many women in my life. We think that people should just get it. Especially our significant others. We don't want to have to tell them certain things, we want them to care enough to just know. Well ladies, that is just not the case! It may be for someone, I'm sure out there in this universe. But as for my relationship and that of many of my friends, men aren't mind readers!

We will have all these issues with things and just bottle them up inside waiting for him to understand our body language or facial expression and lovelies, we will be waiting forever! I had to learn how to speak up about the things that I wanted or the things that made me uncomfortable. One of the biggest mistakes that I would make in my relationship would be in the moments where he asked me "What's wrong?" and I would say "nothing." That is such a huge mistake. Why? Because nine times out of ten, it would be something. I notice that if I think a feeling of mine is not valid, I have a hard time voicing it. I have learned that it is okay to have feelings and really the only way to work through them is to talk about them. But we don't have to feel like our feelings are fact as Myleik Teele often says. But the only way to sort them out and find out what's real and what's not is to express them in a safe environment.

I would just hold all my feelings in until I felt like I had the chance to let it out and then it would turn into such a big spill. I would be pouring out things that happened months ago because I was just suppressing them instead of going through them. But if I would have just discussed it when asked, we probably could have gotten through it a lot quicker and without all the drama.

Now I don't want to confuse you because I said that sometimes you have to work through the emotions first before you actually bring an issue to your partner. That is true. But in communicating effectively, you have the opportunity to say "I am a little upset about something, but I just want to take a second so that I am not speaking out of anger." BOOM! You have still effectively communicated something to your partner without saying "nothing" and leaving them in the dark.

It's the small things that will take you far in your relationships. Most often, it's not the big things that break people apart. It's a combination of the little things that if addressed, probably could have created a smoother path.

Another one of the important things that I had to learn in communicating with my partner is that every disagreement doesn't have to be an argument. I am a loud person by nature. So sometimes an argument would escalate just based off of raising the volume of my voice when communicating a concern. That's something I had to grab a hold of because I noticed my significant other was no longer able to focus on the task at hand once my voice began to raise. His defense was automatically up and neither of us were going to properly hear one another after that.

We have to remember that our body language and tone are important because all those things affect the way our partner receives whatever it is that we are trying to say to them. It took a while for my significant other and I to be able to get an understanding with each other, to be able to voice concerns, or have a disagreement without it escalating. We had to understand one another's cues. But this makes me think of the investment that is necessary when it comes to relationships. We have to invest in learning our partners and many of us simply don't want to invest that much in another person. We're lazy in a lot of ways and want everything to come easily to us. But so much of the start of a relationship is learning a whole heck of a lot about one another and how to co-exist lovingly.

Even still, I have a very hard time making sure what's happening in my mind is not showing on my face. But at least now I am aware. When we are aware, we should be able to adjust. Again, you never hear each other when voices are raised and body language is threatening so nothing is properly resolved in that manner. I feel like I need to drive this point home because way too many of us still think that yelling resolves conflict. Once you start yelling, no one is listening and it will not properly be resolved.

A big part of communicating effectively is also listening! Have you ever heard that saying that we have two ears and one mouth for a reason? I am a very defensive person by nature. I always want to be doing the right thing and saying the right thing, so when someone brings an issue to me about something I may have done or said, nine times out of ten, my guard is already up. This behavior of course trickled into my relationships as well because, hey, that's what happens. We bring our baggage. In constantly being on the defense, I wasn't actually hearing what the other person had to say, I was already putting together my rebuttal.

So there are times where I literally have to remind myself just to listen. To wait and really hear the person out before I even think of what I am going to say next. Sometimes we are distracted by our rebuttal, other times we are distracted by everything else like work, life and if we remembered to do something on our task list. It's important, especially in this day and age to *slow* down and handle one thing at a time. Your partner, your friend, your loved one, deserves your full attention. Try to find the moments to talk when the phones are away, the housework is not an issue, or whatever else could be distracting you from having the real conversations you need to have with loved ones.

It seems like a simple concept that we would be able to speak effectively about what's on our minds to those that we love and adore. But time and time again I have seen that communicating is simply not an easy task for everyone. We are often bound by our past experiences, how we were raised, fear of vulnerability and the list goes on and on. We have all these "things" with us, all this icky stuff that gets in the way of being able to speak our minds in a way that gets the message across clearly to our counterparts.

Remembering things like love believes the best and love is patient and kind, I believe help me to keep an open mind when coming to my partner or loved ones about the things that are on my mind. It took me a long time to realize that my communication kind of really sucked. But in reality, I see now that I have always been a better written communicator than verbal. I often fear making people feel bad with the things that I say or really just have a hard time putting my feelings into words at times. But I feel fortunate enough that most of the people in my life have been patient while I figured it out.

I have even learned that writing out my feelings before bringing them to another person can be helpful. I know it may seem like an extra step. But honestly, it gives me the freedom to just get it all out and then be able to refine it when I bring it to my counterpart. Try it before you frown your nose up at it.

It's not to say that you'll be perfect and that your significant other or whoever will always be receptive to whatever you have to say. But at the end of the day, it's always knowing that you did your best. Knowing that you held up your end of the bargain and the rest you can't control.

Communicating effectively will undoubtedly put you in a better place in your relationships. It allows you to build trust with that person. They can trust that you won't have alternative agendas that you are keeping from them or harboring feelings that could eventually turn into resentment. Resentment is so destructive when it comes to relationships. But who can we blame if we never made our feelings known to the other person? We have to have accountability for the roles that we play in our relationships. Two people contribute to building up or breaking down a relationship and I believe many of us spend a lot of time focusing on the shortcomings of others without ever doing the important internal work we need to do.

Proper communication helps you so that you are not bound by a bunch of emotions and thoughts that you are afraid to articulate. It creates an open environment for your relationship to thrive and grow. If your partner is comfortable, they can share the things that they like and dislike and that gives you a great opportunity to constantly make your relationship better. It gives them the opportunity to make adjustments where needed as well. There will be adjustments to make. Putting two individuals in relationship with one another is not an easy task. You have different ways of thinking, doing things, and loving. The only way to get on one accord is communication.

I still have a ways to go in really being able to communicate everything that I'm feeling. But let me tell you, I've grown leaps and bounds. I was the person who held a lot in. Or if the other person's argument was more compelling, I felt like my feelings were no longer valid. I learned the hard way that my actions just bred resentment and eventually I wasn't going to be able to hold it in any longer. Recently, I have learned that holding feelings in actually causes me to act out in other ways. We're often afraid of the vulnerability it takes to say, when you did x, y, or z, it made me feel this. That is one of the most important phrases I think you can use in a relationship. You will find that when we are not focused on our own emotions in a situation, we will then try to tear down the other person's actions instead. We're afraid to say, you hurt me or to say, I was scared about our future when you did that. So we blame and berate without ever really evaluating what actually took place.

This process of talking and communicating with your partner will not always be comfortable. But most opportunities for growth rarely are. Sure it may be awkward and clunky in the beginning. But setting the tone for the communication in your relationship from the beginning is so important in shaping the rest of the relationship. There are times when I have been so afraid to really put myself out there and share insecurities or fears and I have found every time I have been met with wisdom and encouragement and sometimes a dose of tough love.

Most people want to feel like they are understood. At the crux of life many people just want you to "get them" and that's the case for our partners as well. As much as we want them to understand the things that are important to us, they also want to feel that way. We all want to know that our thoughts and concerns are valued and held in high regard from our partners. In that, we have to learn how to communicate at all times too. Not just when we are upset or angry because that sets a bad expectation in your relationship as well.

As always both people have to be open, willing, and ready to do the work. You will find the balance. When we are able to communicate, we are truthful with something precious to us like our feelings, our thoughts, our visions and we can create a foundation to build upon in love that's stable. A stable foundation will help you withstand the trials and obstacles that will be thrown your way. Know that, because we will *all* go through things. That is inevitable. But those with faulty infrastructure simply won't be able to withstand.

HeartCheck

Chapter Six

- Are you able to confidently complete the phrase, "When you did _____, it made me feel," when it comes to your partner?

- Do you find yourself holding things in and harboring feelings of resentment? How can you work to truly let them go and forgive?

- Can you think of a time you were able to communicate effectively and the result? How can you do that more?

....

"The only way to get on one accord is communication."

SEVEN
DYING TO FLESH AKA KILLING PRIDE

I know that dying to the flesh may sound all spooky but it's really not. The fact of the matter is, we are human! We tend to want to do things that are pleasing to our flesh. But there is a way to tap more into our spirit, which is necessary in order to be able to honestly and truly be able to love without so many limitations. In our own strength we will probably never be able to love people the way we should. I mean what real person would want to love their enemies? That type of thinking takes putting ourselves to the side and really becoming the people God called us to be. Being able to love in this way is often hindered by pride. We are such prideful people, myself included.

I stress pride for a few reasons and the first is because I think so many of us are prideful and we don't recognize it. We don't identify ourselves that way even when our actions showcase it. I didn't think that certain issues I had personally were related to pride at all. But when I took a deeper look and thought about things like the fact that I hate saying sorry, a light bulb kind of went off there.

My significant other of course brought it to my attention. You have to love them for that right? Being able to put the mirror in front of us so that we can occasionally see ourselves more clearly. I just felt that sorry was admitting that I was wrong and in some instances I really didn't feel that I was. But you know what? Sometimes I was wrong and sometimes I was right, but handled it totally wrong. It's okay to be sorry, it's okay to be flawed. And sometimes, it's not even as much about accepting blame as much as raising a white flag that says "I don't want to fight" or "It just isn't that important, let's move on from this."

I didn't realize how afraid I was to be vulnerable and how that related to being prideful as well. After you have been through relationships, life, and various heartbreaks, you build walls. You let fear of those past instances affect how much you let people in. Some may look at that as a tactic of survival in what can be a cruel world at times and I get that to a certain extent. But you can't keep those walls up forever, though pride will certainly try to hold on to them for you. We are full of pride and don't want people to get the "drop" on us or give them the opportunity to hurt us knowing how much we honestly and truly care. But you will never allow yourself true intimacy with a person unless you can indeed learn to be vulnerable with them. Our society views vulnerability as a sign of weakness, not realizing that it takes a lot more strength to be "naked" so to speak with another human being. Really naked, not just revolving around taking your clothes off which can sometimes be the easier part.

Real nakedness is about giving people the real ability to see us. All of us without the facades that so many of us put up on the day to day basis. But there is only so much that you can hide from a person that you are in daily communication with. Eventually they will see you, the real you and hopefully they will be with a person you can trust with that.

We confuse maintaining our dignity with pride and they are

really two different things. Our dignity is being worthy of honor and respect which should certainly be present in all of our close relationships with friends, family, and lovers. Pride, however is linked to self-gratification whether earned or not. Often when we are prideful, we are more puffed up than we really ought to be. My fear of being vulnerable was rooted in pride. If I let my guard down, "what if he hurts me?" "What if I am made to look silly?" Well those are some of the risks that we take in loving others. The best thing that we can do there is have trust. Trust that we have put ourselves around people with good intentions for us and realizing that we all fall short. There will be times when we will be hurt, but the resilience of the heart is mind blowing. We heal and we are able to put our heart on the table again. Being disappointed is not always the end of the world. Keep in mind that you will also disappoint at times and it will help keep things in perspective.

I find pride important to talk about because of how much The Bible talks about it. That indicates to me that pride is a big issue when it comes to human beings and it has been since the beginning of time. It can block our blessings in more ways than one. The other day, I got to thinking about the humility of Jesus and the example we have to look to when it comes to His journey.

God gave His son. Who gave His life for us so that we may live while we were still sinners. When I think of that, I think of his humility. Think of the humble servant he was. The son of God, but allowed himself to be beaten, dragged, ridiculed, and nailed to the cross. The power that must have taken to remain in God's will. It's immeasurable really and a price none of us would have been willing to pay for our fellow man. Yet many of us are so easily offended. At the slightest turn or inkling of disrespect, we fly off the handle or we're out the door. What have we really endured? That is not to take away from people that have been in some really messed up situations. I truly and honestly understand that, but God can even heal and restore you from that, from the unthinkable.

Are we in our own will or the will of God? Is this a situation where you can humble yourself or not? Our pride gets in the way. But tell me, how can we be more prideful than the son of God? Someone who went through the unthinkable and still prayed for his enemies. That is humility. We have to find it. Sometimes it won't be easy for us, sometimes it may hurt, and sometimes it may call for us swallowing our pride to say to another person, "I want you in my life." I want to work things out. I was wrong. I like having you here. What can we do to improve our relationship? When did we become so afraid of that kind of honesty with people that we say we love?

God detests the prideful. Those that have more faith in themselves than they have in Him. Not that we shouldn't have honor, confidence, or standards. But when we are falsely puffed up, when we believe more in ourselves than in Him and His power in our relationships, that is not God's will. When you compare yourself to Jesus, tell me do you think you have the right? We pale in comparison right? So what gives us an attitude of pride? I believe that keeping Jesus in mind when we think about pride, at least in my mind, helps me melt my sense of entitlement and the sense that my love has to be so fiercely earned when God continually gives us His love and we're unworthy.

I do not understand how we think that we can have healthy, flourishing relationships clinging desperately to our fleshly pride. There will be times when loving someone definitely does not feel good. You will be forced to sacrifice at times and to give up something. Sometimes it's the false sense of what you think that you deserve that will get you into trouble.

Nothing is perfect. We are not. Human beings are not. We are going to make mistakes, we are going to royally mess it up from time to time. But we have to learn forgiveness for relationships to last. We have to be willing to put ourselves aside at times. We have to be able to say that we're sorry, that we love one another, that we may not have gotten it right but that we are still willing to try.

There is nothing to be ashamed of here. So often we are trying so hard to keep up with the Joneses'. Not just in material things but also in our relationships. We think if our friends tell us that cheating is a deal breaker in their marriage that it also has to be the same for us. Because what will they think if I take him or her back? Let me tell you something, your relationship is between you and that person. If you spend a lifetime consulting others on what should and shouldn't be acceptable in your relationship, you will never be happy.

Define your own rules and your own boundaries. Don't let your pride get in the way of creating meaningful relationships. I once heard someone say that "Until we die, we cannot live." They were talking about dying within ourselves. Dying to our needs and wants and learning how to put others before ourselves. Love is of the spirit. There is a connection that you have to be able to make there in order to truly love one another with agape love. It's possible, but not when we think that we can do it in our own strength. Are you willing to die to self?

We make people jump leaps and bounds for our love when really it was meant to be given freely. We were created to love. It was the greatest commandment of all because if you dedicate yourself to loving people, you would never break any of the other commandments. Trust is earned, but love should be given. Learning to give others the grace that God extends to us on the daily basis will help our relationships in various arenas flourish. Sometimes that grace will involve pushing our pride aside.

HeartCheck

- Have you let pride affect your relationships? Are you even able to identify your prideful moments?

- Have you ever been afraid to be honest with someone because of how it would make you look?

- Are you self-sabotaging relationships because you are afraid to get hurt?

....

"Until we die, we cannot live."

EIGHT
THE COMPANY WE KEEP

"Walk with wise and become wise, for a companion of
fools suffers harm."
(Proverbs 13:20)

Who are you spending your time with? This is an essential piece
to helping you love on purpose. If you surround yourself with loving, caring, generous people, believe me, it will eventually rub off on
you, period. Have you heard the concept that your life is a reflection
of the 5 people you spend the most time around? Your view on relationships is definitely influenced in a similar way.

Both my father and my significant other are two of the most
generous people I have met. They are honestly the folks that will
give you their last dollar and not really know how they are going to
make it. Though I have chastised them both about this on multiple

occasions, I have truly been impacted by their generosity. I am a more generous person because I know them. I have watched them help others, give their time, lend money and much more. What does that have to do with love? Well, the same goes for love. Are you surrounding yourself with healthy examples of parents that love their children, husbands that love their wives, or believers that show love to strangers? It matters, it matters a lot who we put ourselves around on the daily basis. ALERT: Another decision. There are some folks that you can't avoid in life like co-workers or random people you encounter but who are you with in your spare time, in the moments when you are in control?

We have to get very intentional about our space because whether we recognize it or not the people in our lives have power. We are either being influenced positively or negatively. Not too many things in life are lukewarm. People that we surround ourselves with have power over our moods, our way of thinking, and ultimately the decisions that we make. Have you ever been around a person and just felt drained? That is something to be aware of and something that is affecting your peace and you have to be mindful of that.

Now am I saying that you should only be around one type of person? No. We are supposed to be able to be light in dark places. But you have to be able to refill around other lights or eventually yours will get extinguished. There have been certain times in my own life where I have felt completely empty. I've written blogs, thrown events, orchestrated marketing promotions and poured into others, never taking the time to refill. You can't love on others properly without first being filled with the love of God. And as you continue to love people you will also need to continue to get back into God's presence and be refilled. It's cyclical in that way.

Outside of spending time with God, it's awesome to be around others that will reinforce that type of positive, intentional love. I love being around other loving couples or just positive friends. You would be surprised how much it will affect your own ability to see things clearly in your own relationships. Often I have been guilty of not realizing how great the people I have in my life are until I am reminded by friends who can see the goodness in my situations. It's easy to take the ones you love for granted and positive influences in your life will remind you not to do that. They have the ability to completely change my outlook at times when I may be feeling a little depleted.

We tend to not take the importance of protecting our space as seriously as we should. Especially in the day and age of social media, we are allowing so many negative influences in our lives without even being cognizant of it. We are looking at other people's relationships from a bird's eye view and wondering why we don't have what they have. This is without realizing that we have no clue what people put into their relationships to get joy and happiness out of it. Or we are seeing it one way when in reality their relationship could not be as great as it photographs. We are not being protective of our space. Guard you heart and your timeline, I often say. We tend to be conscious of it more in the real world than in the digital. But everything that we put in front of us has an effect. So be sure your #relationshipgoals are truly those built on a solid foundation and not just what it "looks like."

I'm always shocked when I know people that are in relationships that don't have couple friends. Clearly I have some single friends but often their motives and interests are very different than mine. When you are single a lot of your social life revolves around trying to not be single. So you want to go out, get drinks, and take the town. Which makes complete sense, but when you are not in that mental space because you are in a relationship, it can tend to be a strain on the friendship.

I see sometimes where people are in relationships and keeping a lot of company with single friends and I never really feel like it ends well. Your lives are going to have differences, you just have to be conscious of that and avoid "looking" single because you are out and about with people that are.

The great thing about finding some friends that are couples is that you can spend a lot more quality time with your significant other while hanging out with other people. Find people you both enjoy being around and you get used to having fun together instead of constantly wanting to exclude them from certain parts of your social life. In my own life, we are friends with people who have helped us grow in our relationship based off being real, living examples of what love really looks like. They are not perfect people, but their transparency helps us with pitfalls to avoid and their wisdom at times has helped us navigate tricky spaces in our own relationship.

Am I saying that we shouldn't have single friends? No. Am I saying that you can't have friends that are just your own? No. But I have found that there is a certain clear air to my significant other knowing the people in my life that are close to me. And even though we are not attached at the hip at every waking moment, he is comfortable with the people in my life. Yes we have our own time alone but we also really enjoy the time we spend together.

Setting the expectation is key. For both of us, we came from past relationships where it wasn't as much of a priority to have time spent together. We did a lot on our own and realized it caused a separation that really just caused us to drift apart from our respective exes. So we decided that we wanted a closeness in our relationship together. The great part is we enjoy each other's company and so there aren't many things that you'll see him attend without me by his side and vice versa. That may sound like too much for you, but you just have to come to whatever agreement works with you and your partner.

The bottom line is, who you keep around you, the people that you allow in your space, matter. Be intentional about that. Don't complain about where you are in your life if you are not making an effort to change your surroundings. Why are we keeping miserable, negative, or sometimes jealous people around us? Cut those strings, limit that time because it will affect your ability to love in the way that you want to. Put a pause button on the friends that you know aren't happy and don't want you to be either. That whole saying that misery loves company is true. And I know at times we can be blinded by "friendships" and think people really have our best interest at heart but some people don't. Tap into that spirit of discernment here because I guarantee there have been signs that you probably just ignored.

Iron definitely sharpens iron. The more you are around people who are where you want to be, the better off you are. I know that peer pressure can seem like this thing that goes away after college or so maybe. But you'd be surprised how influenced we still are by our friends even as adults. It's kind of scary.

When you are going through something, you need people who will speak life into your situation. Not people that will just continue to tear it down or join in on your own pity party. You need people around you who can be objective and most importantly tell you the truth even if it's something you may not want to hear. It's so imperative when things may be going awry. Even when things are going well you will want to be around people that build you up. That is everything. A great support system is the key to success in many other parts of life as well as relationships.

It's tough because you hear so many friends get upset if you get into a relationship and can't spend as much time with them. But isn't that really how it should be? Shouldn't friends understand that this person then takes a bit of precedent in your life? Not that you ever kick your friends to the curb, but as your lifestyle changes so will the people you spend time around. For instance, I don't have any children yet. Do you think that I want to spend all my time around new mothers? Nothing against them, but no I don't! I have a different and way more unpredictable lifestyle. I don't have to get a sitter if I want to go out or stay in because of a sick baby. But guess what? When I do have children, I will be seeking out other friends with children because our lifestyles will be more compatible. Well, it's similar in every other area of our lives! We find people that have similar values, passions, and lifestyles so that we can relate on various different levels and most importantly, help each other grow.

Whether it's a couple that is actively contributing to building up your relationship or just an encouraging, like-minded friend, the company we keep can either be a lifeline or a death trap. Community is so important even though we live in a world that will try to make you believe that you can do everything yourself. You just can't. Things get tough and you will want that love and support when it does to keep you encouraged and on the right path in your relationship. It's not about having people that you tell all your business to either. Sometimes you don't even have to discuss specific issues, but seeing how another couple relates to each other can simply be an example to you.

We get to choose what we want our relationships to be. We get to choose our friends and what we want our intimate circles to look like. Hopefully you'll make the wiser decision the more that you read.

Chapter Eight

- Are you spending time with people that are striving towards similar things?

- Have you held on to friendships that you know may be toxic? What is keeping you from letting them go?

- Who do you confide in the most when it comes to your relationships?

··

"The bottom line is, who you keep around you, the people you allow in your space, matter."

NINE
FORGIVING QUICKLY

I once heard my mother say that the key to long lasting relationships is developing a healthy dose of amnesia. The fact is that we will all go through things, for sure whether it's in romantic relationships, friendships, or with family. But in order to love with our whole hearts, we have to be able to not only learn how to forgive, but to forgive quickly.

I distinctly remember one day being out for a picnic with my husband, well he was still my boyfriend at the time. Somehow we got into a spat about where we wanted to actually lay this picnic out, which turned into such a bigger disagreement. Here I was so happy and proud about this whole picnic I put together and we were ruining it by letting our tempers flare about something as stupid as which pier we had in mind to go to.

I remember distinctly thinking, "Well what now?" I didn't want to just go home. But how was I supposed to have this cutesy picnic with him when I literally probably wanted to scratch his eyes out?

But a calm came over me and I thought to myself, do I really want to let this, something so stupid, ruin my whole day? That question has ultimately pulled me out of a lot of the funkiest moods you can imagine. At the end of the day, when we are with someone we love, when we are in a great friendship, or whatever, do we really want something silly to come in between that? I have seen friendships end over not being invited to an event, the fact that someone forgot to return something they borrowed, or simply failed communication where one person took something offensively and never took the time to articulate it to the offender. I always think to myself, "They couldn't have been that great of friends if that tore them apart, right?"

If we ask ourselves, "Is this thing coming between us more important than the friendship and the answer is no, this relationship is more valuable to me, that is a moment where we are able to learn to forgive more quickly and move on with continuing to love that person. I find that the older I get, the less any of the things I thought mattered so much, do anymore.

I talk a lot about forgiveness and it's because it tends to be a very difficult thing for us as people to master. That in addition to communication. We truly harden our hearts towards others and wonder why love can't find its way in and it can be rooted in our lack of trust and forgiveness.

The biggest key to forgiveness is our own accountability for the things that we have done to contribute to the strife. This manifests itself in multiple ways. The first is that we often turn a blind eye to our contribution in the conflicts in front of us. We see what someone has done to us, but we easily ignore anything we could have done to contribute. So all we see is the action from the other person and not the petty thing we said to incite them more, the neglect of the other person's feelings or whatever else we may have added. We judge the reaction and not the action from ourselves that could have contributed to it.

The second way that we struggle in our ability to forgive is that we quickly forget that whether we were wrong in a particular situation or not, we may have been wrong, some time, some place, some way. If we cannot forgive others, we are blocking our opportunity to be forgiven by God. No sorry, we're not perfect and will at some point need forgiveness. Every single one of us will stand in need of grace and forgiveness at some point in our lives. How can He release us from the transgressions we have performed when we are bitter, hateful and have unforgiving hearts?

We cannot ask God for the very thing that we are unwilling to give to someone else. Have you ever been convicted in your spirit that way? You find yourself scoffing at what someone else did but then remember that you are not a perfect person. Often we try to measure things up thinking that what we did wasn't as bad as this other thing. But did you hurt someone? Did you let someone down? At the end of the day, we all fall short and knowing that, accepting that about ourselves will certainly aide in our ability to forgive others.

Forgiveness is honestly more peace for your heart than for the person you are forgiving. When we don't forgive, it takes so much effort to hold on to that angst against another person while they are just continuing with their life. At a certain point you are really giving that person power over your life that they don't deserve when they have done some type of harm to you. I know it may sound like rhetoric, but trust and believe, your forgiveness of others is really for you.

There is also the fact that sometimes we can't forgive others because we can't forgive ourselves. We're strange that way. Our internal battles often reveal themselves vividly in the way that we decide to treat others. When you can't release yourself, you can't release others. Believe me I can attest to that. I mention all the time that I went through a period where I really struggled with forgiving myself for decisions I made. I am the hardest on myself, so when my expectations are extremely high for myself, I also project that onto others. But in accepting my imperfection, in allowing God's forgiveness to really take hold in my heart, I am better able to release others for their same imperfection. Each and every morning I add to my confession:

"Lord, I pray to extend the same grace to people that you extend to me. And Lord I pray to extend the same grace to myself, that you extend to me."

So how do you know when you have really forgiven someone? When you can treat them as if what they did never happened. I remember on various occasions thinking that I had forgiven people but wincing if I heard their name. It took time for me to accept that I hadn't really forgiven them.

As long as you still feel that thing or can't treat someone fairly, you have not forgiven. Think of God as the example. I know he's dope right? Is he constantly reminding us of all the things that we have screwed up? Or does he give us new mercy every single day? Now we will never be as forgiving as God. We are mere human beings with emotions and all that good stuff. But just thinking and acknowledging His mercy is surely a step in the right direction and can begin to soften your heart a bit for those that may have done wrong or hurtful things to you in your past or present.

Many people will say "Well what about when the person keeps doing the same thing over and over again?" There are a couple of things to consider with that. Just because you forgive someone does not mean you have to invite them back into your space. We also have a spirit of discernment and should know when people or situations are just detrimental to our well-being. We have an obligation to guard our hearts, and in that we can't allow people to continually do damage. Let's be honest, we tend to know when someone is really repenting about their behavior and when they are just saying what we want to hear. Repenting involves changing their ways. We just have to learn to be truthful with ourselves when we are giving someone chance after chance to put us in the same predicament. If we are not learning from the situation, then it's tough to trust the process of true forgiveness. You indeed have the ability to forgive a person and they can go on with their life and most importantly, you can go on with yours.

Another factor in forgiveness is knowing that a person is actually acknowledging what they did was wrong and they have a willingness to turn their heart the right way. The key here is a heart of repentance and not remorse. Most often people experience remorse only because they were caught in the wrong act. But repentance acknowledges wrong doing and adds the step of actually trying to change.

It's very hard to forgive someone who doesn't acknowledge that they are wrong. But it's still very possible with God in your corner. Just continue to pray for that person and know that their justice will come from God and not you. They will eventually have to confess all their sin and so will you. So don't let someone who was ugly inside add to your rap sheet because you couldn't forgive. Free yourself of that burden.

As I mentioned, we have to not only forgive, but forgive quickly. Who wants to go through life holding grudges? Who wants every disagreement to turn into a huge ordeal that takes away from a whole day? We don't have forever, our time really is precious and something we can't get back. Someone told me recently that people on their deathbed are never asking for more things or materials, they are normally asking for more time. Forgiving quickly allows you to enjoy the people in your life, to work past their shortcomings, and make the most of your time together. Sometimes a lifetime doesn't seem like enough to spend with those you love so don't waste it. What will it serve you to show how long you were able to stay mad? Forgive them, because in the process, you will get your peace back as well.

For my parents, you are also setting an example for your children. No I don't have kids yet, but I promise you I understand how important the influence of our parents are when it comes to relationships. I may not have kids, but I do have parents! And a lot of the way that they related to one another is how I found myself relating to my partner as well. Create that loving atmosphere and show your children the importance of forgiveness. Show them that even though mommy and daddy may disagree at times that your love for one another will always outweigh who was right or wrong.

In our day to day relationships, what if we stopped adding everything up and compiling things? I thought to myself the other day, what if you treated each day like it was brand new in your relationship? When you say that you forgive, when you have addressed an issue, it's best to leave it there. If you have resolved it, then you shouldn't be allowed to hold it against the person forever. So many times in relationships we like to say that we forgive the person because it sounds good. But at every waking chance we get, we are attempting to make them pay for the hurt that they may have caused. But that is hell for your partner and whether you realize it or not, it's hell for you too. To be constantly reliving hurt and pain and the loss of trust is not good for your health and eventually it will alienate your partner as well.

Lately I have found myself repeating, "love keeps no record of wrong." There have been things in my own relationship that I thought that we worked through, but I can see still manifest at certain points. It will come out. When you have not truly forgiven your partner, it will reveal itself in your behavior. We are typically not as good of actors or actresses as we think. Get it all out there and then work towards forgiving one another. Ask for God's help in eliminating the record that you have been keeping of their wrongs because true love is not like that. It will take some time to get there, but again, all things are possible with God. So I will be working right alongside you to make sure that once an issue has been addressed, that it is expunged.

You may forgive someone before they are able to really gain your trust back and I get that. Often times forgiveness is quick and the trust is what takes time to be rebuilt. So take your time. Forgiving quickly doesn't mean not taking the time you need to process. Sometimes we are just freaking out over small stuff like where to have a picnic which does need to be forgotten quickly and other times there are way bigger issues happening and wounds that will take more time to heal. But remember to have mercy on that person the same way God has mercy on us each day when he forgives us over, and over, and over again. Maybe you have never been in need of forgiveness, but I know that I have and so that makes me so much more willing to forgive the people that I say I love in my life. If you can show me a perfect person, I'll wait.

HeartCheck

Chapter Nine

- Are you quick to cut people off and be unforgiving of even small violations?

- Do you consider your own need for forgiveness when deciding to forgive someone else?

- Who do you need to forgive in your life and how is it affecting your relationships?

....

"Love keeps no record of wrong."

TEN

OVERCOMING FEAR

Fear can be crippling and most definitely stands in the way of us creating robust relationships in all areas of our lives. So many of us are afraid! Afraid of the unknown, afraid of getting hurt, and afraid of the rate of failure in relationships we've seen before us. How would we move differently if we were no longer afraid? This is a big question not only in love but in our lives in general.

It's easier said than done for sure. I struggle with fear on the regular basis, believe me. But I also realize that fear and faith can't occupy the heart at the same time. We are not given a spirit of fear but of peace, love, and a sound mind. (2 Timothy 1:7) So we have to work at every turn to combat fear from prohibiting our ability to love on purpose.

Fear in relationships often reveals itself in our lack of trust. We are afraid to be hurt and so we build up those walls I keep mentioning and we only share pieces of ourselves hoping to create something good, something whole. And that is where so many of us fail. The problem with that is that we will never experience the fullness of love when we shield ourselves from it because of fear. Though ultimately we believe we are protecting ourselves, we're really disabling ourselves. God is our protector. Not just in this ethereal way either. No he is not going to literally come down and shield us. But he gives us discernment, he works through people, and the Holy Spirit convicts us at very important times. When we lean more into Him as our protector, we become less involved in working so diligently to protect ourselves. When we walk in tandem with Him, we know when he's telling us to back off and we know when he's telling us, this is safe.

Loving people can be a scary thing. People are unpredictable and anyone with sense might proceed with caution. That's just what's real. So when we talk about having to learn to trust, it's really with a spirit of discernment of who is really trustworthy. I will always tell you to guard your heart in that way. But the reality is, a lot of us just take that way too far. We not only guard our hearts, we have it wrapped in titanium with a lock and key. We are just too set in our ways, too deep in a spirit of distrust that we are too afraid to let ourselves get there in love.

In my personal life, when I am afraid, I have started to think in that moment about the worst possible outcomes of my fear. Really fear is just this irrational anticipation of something that has yet to happen. It could even be something in your past that actually happened and your fear is based on the anticipation of it happening again with no real proof that it will. Face the worst case scenario in your mind and slowly you will be able to combat those fears.

For instance, so many people are afraid of their mate cheating. The worst case is that yes it will hurt and be terrible, but guess what? You will live through it. No one wants to experience that, but it won't take you out of here barring disease or any of the serious things like that because I would never play with those things. When you face that reality and say to yourself, the worst thing that can happen is I will find out and I will be able to dodge that bullet because that person is not meant for me anyway. We then have a better chance of moving past the fear.

There is so much wrapped into that scenario including the fact that we often blame ourselves and the shame that comes along with it. But when we are whole, often we can move away from a toxic experience and say, "that had everything to do with them and who they are and maybe a little to do with me and who I am." Our devastation is often based in what we think was wrong with us. But someone's inability to see our worth is their problem, not ours. We could honestly live in "what ifs" all day. What does that do besides get us riled up about things that may never actually happen?

We have to just be better at feeling the fear and moving on from it. More and more I feel like this notion is what courage is made of. Feeling the fear and doing it anyway because what's on the other side is greater than the fear. I want to urge you to be courageous enough to love though you may be afraid. We can't eliminate fear. I think it's part of our humanity. But if this person gives you nothing to worry about, why are you worrying about it? And if they do give you things to be worried about and that you're suspicious of, why are you sticking around?

What we often don't realize is how powerful the things we mediate on can be. The thoughts that are constantly on your mind are in your future. Your thoughts are shaping your reality. What you think you are capable of, the type of significant other you want, how you think someone will treat you can all begin to shape your reality. If we are constantly fearful of what will happen in our relationships, it can begin to manifest. It's crazy to me how fearful we are to just believe the best at times. The world is so jaded and people's perception of love is so negatively depicted that we begin to believe the worst as the norm. We want to beat life to the punch of the worst case scenario. But we have to be diligent in remaining optimistic. When we change our thoughts and our outlook, we begin to change our reality. And what we believe is possible is what we will attract to our lives.

So if you are constantly talking about divorce rates and the lack of good men or women, and that it's impossible to find something good these days. Guess what, that's exactly what it's going to be. What is on your mind and in your mouth is in your future. If you meditate on the fear of everything that can happen, you will never find the fullness of love. Fear and doubt is just a tactic of the enemy and the sooner you realize that, the better off you will be. He doesn't want you to find love and get married and be under the covering of God. So he will play to every fear that you make known and make you think that it is impossible to find something real and something true.

Kicking the fear won't happen on its own either. Again that idea that we must be intentional in our love presents itself. I find that sometimes I don't want to believe the best because what if I am let down? But do you see how short you can sell yourself with that mindset? Live with the fact that things in life and love can work out or not, our relationships can be hurtful and learning lessons or full of joy. This is simply a part of this life thing that we do. Be anxious for nothing including fearing that the worst will always happen in your relationships with other people.

Everything in life needs balance. Guard your heart, but not so much that nothing can get in or out. Be prayerful about your fears. With His help you will be able to overcome all the past hurts, damage or whatever else is holding you back from truly being able to love others the way we were truly made to love. But you have to be able to face those fears. Be honest about them and acknowledge that you are just afraid. Vocalize that to your partner so that they may be able to adjust accordingly in ways to make you less fearful. And don't be afraid to pour your heart out to God about them as well. His strength is perfected in our weakness. (2 Corr. 12:9) If there is anyone or thing or being that you can be completely vulnerable with it is God. He will never break your heart. So pour it out, do it afraid, and let His goodness give you the strength and courage you need.

HeartCheck

+ Are you considering how to determine who is trustworthy to be in a relationship with or just jumping in head first?

+ Have you allowed the "What ifs" to keep you from actually trying in love?

+ Have you ever been truly honest about your fears in love with God?

....

"Fear in relationships often reveals itself in our lack of trust."

ELEVEN

LOVING YOURSELF

In various ways I know it sounds cheesy or cliché, but loving yourself is truly one of the most important steps in learning to love on purpose. We can't miss it. But many of us do and continue to struggle in our relationships with other people and have no idea why.

It is nothing easy to do. But I hope that I have stressed enough that love is not always an easy thing. I have constantly struggled with knowing that I am enough within myself and it has on occasion caused strife and insecurity in certain relationships. Getting ourselves in line personally is key to establishing healthy relationships with our loved ones.

I heard Steve Furtick say recently, "When you like yourself, it doesn't matter who on the outside may dislike you." Maybe I am the only one but honestly and truly liking and accepting myself whole heartedly has taken a lot more time than I imagined. Maybe we have to accept that it's somewhat of a lifelong process. Truly knowing and being comfortable with the core of who you are as a person is so necessary in life in general and certainly in love.

So how do we begin the process of actually loving ourselves? Well, I believe that it starts with knowing exactly how much God loves you. When we look at His love for us, it is reassurance that we are not here by accident but with intended purpose. Knowing who and whose you are in life is a giant step in being able to identify the truth of your value. You are a King's kid and should therefore act and be treated accordingly.

We often let how we grew up or who are parents were define us. But regardless of upbringing we have a Heavenly Father that loves and thinks the world of us. Sometimes that is all you may have to hold on to but the good news is that it's all you really need. Don't worry about your past because at any point in life when you accept Christ, you can become new.

At the time when I got saved, I was going through a lot of different life transitions. I was so hard on myself for allowing certain things to happen in my life and I was a little afraid. But as I sat under the word of God, I thought to myself, how could God really love me? There are all these things wrong with me, all these things that I have screwed up. But still His love was unfailing.

There is an interview with Maya Angelou from one of Oprah's shows. Dr. Angelou talks about a phone conversation that she was having with a pastor, I believe. He told her, I want you to say, "God loves me." And she said it but he asked her to say it again. She repeated it over and over until it hit, deeply. "God. Loves. Me." And in the interview you can see her get swept up in the emotion and it had the same exact effect on me. I tried it. Over and over. "God loves me." I felt unworthy and so fortunate at the same time. This here is a powerful thing to understand.

Getting that revelation of love changed my life. It took a really long time too for it to really sink in. But once I got it, I knew that there was nothing a person could tell me to get me to think different. I couldn't allow anyone to mistreat me, knowing how special I was to God. I couldn't even allow me to mistreat myself. You really have to be able to get that deep down inside your heart. You have to know your worth, it outweighs any worldly possession. We have to remember that at all times. What we don't think we deserve, we will never be able to accept from another person. If you are not comfortable with the fact that you deserve love, you are susceptible to anything that someone dresses up and calls love.

God, myself, others. That is the order. When you try to do them out of order, it just doesn't work. Our love for Him shapes how we love ourselves. If we simply love ourselves first, we are putting ourselves higher than we ought to. And if we try to love others first, the same is happening. Loving God will show you how to love yourself and in turn, others. Work on the vertical relationship and you will be able to extend horizontally.

One of the next steps is learning how to embrace your flaws in the midst of the refinement process. There is a quote that I love from Sophia Bush that says:

> "You are allowed to be both a masterpiece and a work in progress, simultaneously."

You are not perfect and never will be, but think about how much God loves you in spite of that. If he can love you flaws and all, then you can love yourself the same way! We tend to take on this heaviness about the things that we may want to work on or things that we need to improve. But every single person on this planet is working on something. Or if they aren't, they should be. So you just have to learn how to appreciate the good and the bad.

I am a stickler for growth. It's like something that I am constantly focused on. And that may seem like an admirable trait outwardly, but sometimes I have had to check myself in that process. I will never stop wanting to be better. I mean, I am in heavy pursuit of more Christ-like characteristics in my life. But God also knew exactly what he was doing when he made me, so I always have to keep in mind that as much as I want to grow, I am also fearfully and wonderfully made. As I pursue the best version of me, I also have had to learn how to be comfortable with me in the process.

Changing how we talk to ourselves in our thoughts, is also big one. We, myself included, are often our own worst enemies. We have to begin to shift our language on purpose about ourselves. So things like positive affirmations and life mantras to encourage ourselves are essential in this process. Sure you may feel silly at first, but I promise you that what you affirm you will truly begin to believe. We're not always as complex as we like to think. We are the summation of our repeated behaviors for better or for worse.

I know it may be hard to start on your own so here are a few of my favorite ways to affirm myself. And these work whether you are a woman or a man.

I am a person of integrity.

I am the head and not the tail.

I am above only and not beneath.

I am the righteousness of God.

Christ is in me.

I am enough.

I am kind.

I am sensitive to the Holy Spirit.

Of course many of mine are rooted in faith, but you honestly have to be able to use what works for you. Just make sure that you have your arsenal to use in those times when you just don't believe in yourself. If you don't take the time to affirm yourself, you will always be looking for someone else to. And that's how we get into trouble. That's how the first person to tell us that we're valuable becomes our world when maybe they weren't deserving of that title.

These issues are very real and the cause of a lot of toxic relationships that are eating away at our spiritual wellness. Whether it feels silly or not, I promise you that it helps. Just takes some getting used to.

At times I will literally take a negative thought about myself and turn it around into a positive. It's so easy to get down on yourself so you have to be really conscious of when it's happening. This is a deliberate and intentional way of building a solid foundation of self-love. Anything built on a solid foundation will always have the best chance to last.

At the end of the day, someone who has difficulty liking themselves is going to have a lot of trouble valuing the needs of another person. How can you value the person you are in relationship with if you do not value yourself? So not only do we have to be able to learn to love ourselves, we have to be able to identify when the actions of another are indicative that they may have low self-esteem as well. If you love yourself but are in love with someone who doesn't love themselves, they will not value you, and they will not treat you the way that you should be treated.

"Be careful when a naked man offers you a shirt."
–African Proverb

I love this quote because it illustrates the caution we should use in taking anything, including love from a person who doesn't have it for themselves.

For some people it takes getting to know themselves a little better before getting into anything serious with another person. Others can learn how to love themselves in the process, but you have to evaluate that for yourself. Honestly, how can you expect someone to treat you better than you treat yourself? Seems silly right?

We tend to place our value so far in the hands of others which is so dangerous. When we allow someone outside of God to define our value, what happens when they do not act accordingly or the relationship ends? We automatically question our value. But I am here to tell you that someone cheating or deciding that they don't want to honor you and treat you well is not a basis of your value as a person. That's why this step of learning to love yourself is crucial. I have seen people crushed for years because a relationship didn't work out and it was tied to their value and view of themselves being based on a relationship. Relationships are amazing things, but they should not be the source of your joy or your value. Only God gives us that and it's so important to remember.

Having Godly confidence in who you are will never allow you to let someone talk down to you, treat you like an option instead of a priority or accept anything less than their love and respect. It will certainly never allow you to play second fiddle to someone else, which is always a red flag, I don't care how you try to spin it. Get this one, you do not love yourself if you are allowing someone to keep you on the back burner while they are in another relationship.

I often see such a false sense of confidence in many of today's younger generations. They are puffed up on ego, but it's fairly easy to see through the façade. Their words say, I love myself and my body and my being, but their actions say something totally different. The fact that someone will sleep with any man or woman that gives them just a bit of attention. The fact that they bully and hate on their peers. The fact that they don't take pride in how they look, and the list goes on. Arrogant on the outside, but hurting and dying on the inside with no one paying attention to what's really going on. Arrogance is simply faith in ourselves and our own ability while confidence is our faith in what God can do through us. It's easier than you think to see the difference.

When I think about the way I have been treated in my relationships, it's because even though there are moments when I am unsure of myself, I am ultimately confident in what I bring to the table. No one can come to my door with anything less than respect and honor because I simply do not entertain it. I am confident in God and who he has made me. I am confident that if one thing doesn't work out, I can find something else that may be more beneficial to me. That is the mindset that is so crucial to bring to relationships. After things ended that I thought would last forever, I realized no matter how much I loved someone, life could indeed go on without them. That doesn't mean you don't fight for your relationship or try your best when you have something worthwhile, but you will survive.

We have to stop faking it. We have to really do the work that it takes to appreciate ourselves the same way we appreciate everything else around us and it starts from within. Changing our thinking, rehearsing what God says about us, encouraging ourselves, and spending enough time with ourselves to appreciate all we have to offer. We have to fight the spirit of comparison that says that we are not as good as another person. This is the work and the diligence that it takes to love ourselves and it will not just happen by osmosis. More than likely it will be a continuous process and not just something that we can throw on cruise control.

In turn, our relationships will flourish. Two people with healthy images of themselves will undoubtedly be able to love and respect one another. When we are comfortable with who we are, we will never want to downplay others who look like us. We'll have better relationships with our significant others, family, co-workers, even strangers. We won't manipulate and hurt our significant others because we are confident in who we are. We won't stand for anything less than excellence because we accept that we are King's kids. Begin this important work and watch things begin to turn around for you.

HeartCheck

Chapter Eleven

- Have you ever tried positively affirming yourself to help with your own self-image?

- Are you placing your personal value into the success of your relationship?

- What work are you doing to help manifest self-love?

....

"What we don't believe we deserve, we will not be able to accept from others."

TWELVE

BUILDING TRUST

Building trust sounds simple when we say it, but many of us know that this can be one of the most difficult things for us to do. Trust is the belief that someone or something is reliable, honest, or effective. But more simply defined than practiced. Here is this huge word that honestly is one of the biggest anchors in a solid relationship. Yet we struggle with trust. So how can we be intentional when it comes to trust?

First, I want to be clear that when we talk about trust, it's not just in regard to whether someone will be faithful to you or not. Trust shows itself in many different areas in relationships outside of that. We have to trust that someone will be sensitive to our feelings, trust that they will be there for us when we need them, trust that they will uphold their financial obligations, and the list really goes on. Relationships take trust in many different areas. You are relying on that person to take this commitment seriously. Not just the commitment of a romantic relationship but even in friendships and relationships with family. We are saying "we are in relationship" and trust is something we want to attach to that automatically.

How many of you realize that trust is all about building a track record? There are not too many of us that would automatically trust a stranger with $100 of our money, right? We may barely trust some people we know with $100 of our money. So when in relationships, it takes time to be able to build that type of foundation with another person.

But often times we dive into relationships head first, trusting essentially "strangers" with things more valuable than that $100, like our bodies. We allow people into our personal space, our lives, and our bodies without building any trust and then look perplexed and confused when we begin to create our own track record of trusting someone we never should have in the first place. Then years down the road we finally wake up and have hardened our hearts towards being able to trust anyone. It becomes a vicious cycle.

The first step in building trust is allowing it time to manifest. Again, it makes me think about being in relationship with God. When you are first getting to know Him, you first go to him with simple things. "Lord can I get this job?" "Lord can you keep me safe while I travel," and the like. As He begins to reveal himself to you more and more, your relationship gets deeper. He shows you time and time again that He will come through and so you begin trusting Him with more each time. You trust him with things like finances, career goals, your significant other, your children and slowly begin leaning on Him in every aspect of your life. You trust that He will keep those things and that He will always have your best interest at heart.

The same goes for us building relationships in the natural. It takes a while to trust people. They have to show you that they will come through time and time again. We cannot just expect to trust folks that we have known for 6-months that are clearly just on their best behavior, because aren't we all in the beginning? We have to give it time for us to be in more situations together to see how they react, and see who they are truthfully when not on this trial period. Sometimes it takes a while to see the "real" person come out. When we are rushing into things, we haven't even experienced enough with that person to know who they really are. If you are experiencing one another in the same setting over and over, you will never be privy to what variables can introduce about a person's characteristics.

What do I mean by that? Well, if all we ever do is get together at your house to play video games and order pizza. I may never know how rude you are to servers in a restaurant. If all we have ever done is have fun together, I have no idea how you actually react to serious situations. That's why time becomes so important. I am not saying that everyone has to be together years and years first before they can have a successful relationship, but I am saying that sometimes we simply don't give ourselves enough time to truly learn the interworkings of another human being.

Once the process of getting to know someone under various circumstances runs its course, we are apt to be a little more trusting. Trust tends to be the result of a lot of the small things adding up and that takes time.

Trust also takes humility. There is that important word again. We have to know our own limitations and shortcomings in order to be able to trust another person. When we see our humanity, we tend to be a lot more trusting of that in others. We trust that they may not have meant something they said maliciously or that they actually will come through on something that they said they would help us do. We realize that we have to learn to depend on others at some point because we can't do it all ourselves without anyone, ever. Like the legendary Dr. Angelou said, "Nobody, but nobody can make it out here alone."

Trust can be scary. It's important to remember that. Some of us think that there are supposed to be guarantees in relationships. There are not. I think that once you can wrap your head around that, you end up a lot better off. Often we want to control the outcome so bad that we can't trust the process. Loving another person can be a gamble, but you do your best to improve the odds in the selection process. Who you decide to give your heart to or to allow into your space is important. Be aware of that and what that decision could mean for your future and well-being.

We also have to remember that sometimes people will simply do dumb stuff! I know, real layman's terms, but have you ever just felt that way? Like "man, that was stupid, why would they do that?" But you know what? You will also do some dumb stuff. I would bet on that. We all make mistakes to a certain extent. We cannot be unforgiving of that and taking our trust away at every whim. I am not talking about when someone is intentionally being a jerk, but there will be times when we hurt one another unintentionally and we have to learn to be able to bounce back from that.

Another important factor when it comes to trust is to remember that it can be rebuilt. I don't care what the "world" says about it. They will make you believe that once the trust is gone the relationship is over. But I have seen with my own two eyes trust be broken in a relationship and the two parties had the ability to overcome it. I have seen couples go through the ringer and come out better and stronger on the other side. It is a process, it will be work, and it will take time, but it is indeed possible. All things through Christ are. If you are both willing, it can happen for sure.

The most important piece to this whole trust thing is the fact that it takes vulnerability. I don't know where it has come from, but this is a generation that does not like to be vulnerable. We salute hashtags like #wastehistime because we've been hurt. So, it's difficult for us to say to others, I want you in my life or you add to my life because you're here. We're afraid to trust others with those emotions and feelings.

To be able to say, "That hurt me," or "When you do this it makes me feel …" is letting someone else know that what they do affects your emotional well-being. The lack of trust is the feeling of not wanting another person to have that type of power over you. When you cannot properly communicate with someone you love, you do not trust what happens with the information once it's leaves you for whatever reason. It's important to get to the root of that.

We're so used to being all "I don't need you for anything" that it's hard to make that switch in our minds. Well, at least some of us. Your problem may not be vulnerability but I have seen so many people, men and women alike, create walls while in relationships, never fully letting the other person in. In my humble opinion, it will never really work that way. Even if it does for some time, eventually it won't.

We have to trust our instincts. Trust that we made the decision to be with a person whose intent is never to hurt us, even though we're human and the fact is, we're going to hurt each other sometimes. This sentiment to me magnifies "Love believes the best." (2 Corr. 13). When you are just dating, sure guard your heart. You can't let any Joe Smoe or Sally into your heart space in that way. But I am talking about once you are walking in true relationship with another person.

I think our capacity to trust like love in general also comes from what we think we deserve. So many of us can't even trust ourselves. Not specifically in our relationships but in our lives in general. We don't trust that we're doing the right thing, we don't trust our talents, or we don't trust our decisions. This is projected into our relationships and our ability to trust other people as well.

Recently in a conversation, I realized that part of my apprehension and inability to move on from a particular subject was deeply rooted in my lack of trust for myself. Sometimes I am literally afraid that I will lose interest in relationships because that has been something that has happened to me in the past. Whether it be friends or romantically, this fact that at certain points people can be the closest thing to you and then not, really bothers me.

I realized that some of my trust issues with others comes from my inability to trust that I myself can be what the other person needs me to be long-term. If I am afraid that I will somehow lose interest, then it becomes a fear for me that they may lose interest in me as well. Does that make sense? If I can't even trust myself, how can I truly trust another person? It's as if I have this apprehension that none of us know what we're capable of and so I always tread with caution. Which I, myself am working through.

I have found that when it comes to dealing with people and trusting, I also have to involve God in the process. "God is my protector." Every morning I have a confession that includes this. It's not about putting all of our trust in people because that will fail us every time. But it's trusting that God will indeed protect us and equip us with the discernment to protect ourselves. But you have to be in line with Him to hear that. You have to walk with Him closely to be able to discern who you can and cannot trust.

And it's important to remember in this area that we are not victims to our past. We don't have to be victim to what our mommas didn't do or our daddies or what we have lacked in ourselves in the past. We get the opportunity in each relationship to decide how we are going act and what we are willing to give. It's fear again rearing its ugly head and keeping you from the flourishing in love the way that you really want to in your life when you become distrusting. You are letting fear dictate your ability to trust and it's a dangerous thing. We all want to be trusted and when the person on the other end feels that they aren't, it's hurtful to them as well. It's damaging to both parties to be in a relationship where you don't trust the other person or to be the person on the other end who doesn't feel trusted. This often just leads down a terrible road because lack of trust incites lots of detrimental behaviors.

We struggle with trust. Many of us do. But it's something we can work on for sure. It's something we can mend in our actions and in the decisions we make about who we love intimately. The key here really is being able to identify the different ways that trust plays out. It's not always about "Do I believe you are where you say you are." Most often it's saying, "I have given you something so precious, my heart, can I trust you with it?" Are you starting to see here how many decisions are involved in how we love one another?

HeartCheck

Chapter Twelve

- Do you think that your lack of trust is rooted in pride and ego?

- Do you honestly trust yourself?

- What past experiences are you allowing to dictate your ability to trust?

....

"Trust shows itself in many different areas in relationships."

always easy, but it's necessary.

We also think we can have it our way, all the time, which is pretty childish. Although, truth moment, I have definitely felt that way. "Don't people realize that if they all thought like me, the world would be a better place?" That's a joke but many of our actions showcase this mindset and it's an unrealistic expectation. It sounds ridiculous when we say it, but our actions show this all the time. You nag because he took a longer route to get to the grocery store than you would have taken. He's annoyed because you're a bit more fragile with the children and he thinks you should be tougher on them. We push ourselves onto one another instead of being able to acknowledge and appreciate the differences and then come to a mutual understanding of how we would like to move forward. Again, communication is everything here. When we say, "This is how I view things," or "This is how I would like this to be handled, but what's the middle ground?" These are the important conversations that are often missing from our relationships.

So what does compromise look like in relationships? Well it could be things like splitting up the holidays so that each family gets quality time with you and in many cases the children. It's going to check out his favorite band even though you think it's noise. It's going to the ballet because you know it's her favorite even though it makes you want to poke your eyes out. It's taking the kids this time so that she can go out and enjoy herself or not complaining every time he wants to hang out with his boys. It's knowing I can't have my way every moment of every day. This is the constant give and take that takes place. Yes, sometimes it's tiring and you may even get a little weary, but it's worth it. And honestly when you are truly in love with another person, it shouldn't even feel like such a chore. One thing I love about my relationship is that we genuinely like to be around one another. So no matter if it's something we're crazy about or not, we are just content to be with each other. Whether I am tagging along with him to a gig or if he is helping me with one of my events, we do it because we want to, not out of obligation. We like to make each other happy. We know what that support means to the other person.

Sometimes we'll see that we have to put our immediate needs to the side for a period of time while we let our partner work through something. Or physically a man may have to work a job he doesn't like that pays well to give his wife the time she needs to finish school. There are so many instances of compromise that we will face in life. One of the most important things that I feel I have learned in coming of age is that my life is not as much about me as I may have thought. As a child, it's so easy to be self-centered because everything is centered around your parents or elders catering to your every need. But real life, this adult life, involves being a player in a bigger plan. That's how it helps to think of relationships. The relationship is the plan and sometimes you have to play your part.

At one of my Dear Love Brunches, we had a very interesting discussion rooted in how we are able to decipher whether we are compromising or settling. It yielded very interesting perspective with most of us realizing that there are some core elements that we need in a relationship and that the rest may indeed be negotiable. Give and take comes to mind again. Settling is rooted in thinking that you have taken what you could get instead of the best that may have been available. But I have learned that most often we end up being with a person with qualities that are a lot more of what we need than what we may have thought we wanted. Compromise in my estimation, lands somewhere in between that realization. You have to give something to get something. I feel like that is one of the most basic principles of life in general.

Often we feel like we are giving so much and not even thinking about the fact that the other person is giving as well. We can be short sighted in that way. Compromise is not about settling. Compromise is about the realization that we all have crap with us and that it takes work to get two completely different people with completely different backgrounds to work together on one accord. It's a basic understanding to me. The process will take time. Some of us will be better with compromise than others. Some of us will learn that we are too compromising and have to find the balance. But it's a process and a journey and hopefully one that you can figure out together without falling apart.

No relationship in my estimation can flourish without compromise. When each person is giving, it creates an atmosphere where no one feels cheated or that they are ending up with the short end of the stick. They're not feeling resentment because things are always the other person's way. If you are not willing to bend, I think you need to evaluate whether you really want to be in a relationship or not because that's what it takes. Real relationship takes work and selfish people need not apply. Unfortunately, there is no way around it or there is but I just haven't found it yet. Let me know if you do. But in the meantime, it will take giving something of yourself and your partner giving something of themselves to find a medium ground where both of you can be happy and fulfilled. That's the ultimate goal.

HeartCheck

Chapter Thirteen

- Have you been guilty of wanting it your way all the time?

- What is your biggest set-back when it comes to compromising?

- Are you able to identify when the compromise may seem one-sided? Are you over compromising?

....

"The relationship is the plan and sometimes you have to play your part."

FOURTEEN
UNREALISTIC EXPECTATIONS

Where are you getting your idea of what your relationship should look like from? TV, movies, reality shows, Jay-Z and Beyoncé? I think you see where I am going with this. We often base our ideas of how relationships should be on everything except for the two people that are in them. I want to bring death to the fairytale and the #relationshipgoals hashtag. I know, so harsh but it's for our own good, I promise you.

I'm a sucker for a good romance film like the best of them. I mean seeing people swept off their feet and the endings tied up in a nice neat little bow, how can you resist? But the truth here is, life is not the perfect romance film. Not even close. Real relationships often show the good, bad and the ugly. With that, we have to learn how to set more realistic expectations for ourselves and for our partners.

Realistic doesn't mean settling either. So many of us are so afraid that we will settle for less than we deserve so we create an unrealistic bar for what we want in a partner. Let's not get those two things confused. You can still have an exciting, passionate, loving relationship while maintaining a realistic outlook on the things that you will face. When we set the bar to impossible, all we will be met with is disappointment. Superman was a fictional character and so was Claire Huxtable, remember that. Not that there aren't great men and women out here, but compared to our fictional ideals they will never compare.

Movies often seem to capture the falling in love thing really well. It harps on the emotions that we feel when we are infatuated with one another. You know, when things are not too serious but you're really having a good time with that person and you always find your way through the small tiffs. They show the moments when everything about that person is just adorable to you including their flaws. But what happens when the years really begin to take their toll? When the real life challenges and the curve balls come into play? One thing that we know for sure is that life can get hard and sometimes trying to maintain a healthy relationship in the midst of that can seem impossible. Movies rarely show you what's happening years down the road when the real work is necessary.

See a film has to have a climax. The point of the highest tension or most exciting part. That tends to be the one point when you are not sure if the couple is going to make it or not. You are shown one obstacle, maybe two if they're feeling generous. Then most often they make it past it or they find someone else and they live happily ever after. But how do you sustain obstacle after obstacle, blow after blow and remain standing? It starts with knowing what to expect when you say that you love someone.

In my conversations with various people, I find that their struggles in the dating process are often rooted in unrealistic expectations. They want their counterpart to have it all together, be a mind reader, cook and clean, be sexy, charming, rich, and perfect. How do we expect all these things from another mere human? And do we have all the things together in our own lives that we are looking for? Our vision is 20/20 when it comes to someone else and what we expect from them, but gets all blurry when we have to hold ourselves to the same standards. In most cases, I find that you are what you attract. So if your expectation is to attract someone who has it all going on, it's probably a lot easier to attract that if you do too. It's an unrealistic expectation to create a laundry list of wants and you only have 2.5 things on the list going for yourself.

We also can be unrealistic in the moments when we put more weight on certain things that happen in relationships than others. Our partner will do something that we think is the end of the world, but we neglect some of the things that we may have done to them as well. But the fact of the matter is, we all screw things up in different ways. To take it biblical, we all sin and one sin doesn't outweigh the other. You didn't like the way he ignored you, but you continue to nag. She said something unforgiveable but you incited her. We fault someone for their indiscretions and completely absolve ourselves of the things that we may have contributed to drive them there. That's unrealistic.

I don't want you to misunderstand me. It's not that it's unacceptable to have expectations. We should all have expectations for our relationships and be able to effectively communicate them to our partners or potential partners. And your expectations may not be the same as mine. But we need to evaluate whether we are basing those expectations on what we truly want and need or what our friends, family, or society is telling us that we need. Getting caught up in the "world's" view of our relationships can be extremely detrimental. It takes some soul searching, quiet time and reflection to drown out the voices of others and really take an inventory of what we need to make us happy in a relationship. Do you require a lot of attention? Do you want to have a designated date night every week? Do you want to get married? Do you want to have children? These are real expectations that are so essential to communicate in relationships. We get caught up in a lot of other things and never ask these types of real questions.

We are too often in the pursuit of perfection whether we want to admit that to ourselves or not. One of the most important things that I learned in my own journey is that we all have one thing or three or twenty that won't necessarily be favorable about ourselves. In the dating process, we are constantly trading off shortcomings for other shortcomings until we find the right mix that works for us because no one is perfect. I once heard someone talk about long term relationships by saying, "who will you be able to stand, in a room, with no one else, years down the line?" Who will you be able to stand? I know it sounds so anti-romantic. But really that's what it comes down to because one person will not have it all. It doesn't mean that you won't have amazing experiences and a life full of love, but it's breaking it down to something really digestible. Who do you want to do life with?

What's most important to you? What are the core values of what you want in a counterpart in your life? Is it family? Financial stability? A loving, caring kind heart? Robust social life? What is it? Get it down on paper somewhere, what are the most important things that you are looking for? And let's narrow it down to 5 core values, because of course we could probably fill books on books about every single thing we want from a person in a relationship.

One of my core values has been a willingness to grow. I believe that when a person is willing and dedicated to growth, they have the ability to fill every other one of my needs. It's really about being a witness and support to a person as they grow into who God has called them to be. Best believe that who God called them to be will be better than anything you could have thought up on your own.

When we are unrealistic about what we expect, we end up frustrated, disappointed, and feeling lonely even if we are with someone.

We are only responsible for who we are, what we attract, and what we allow. There are so many beautiful people that you may be missing out on in your life because your checklist is all off. We are in our own way when we not only have unrealistic expectations, but fail at being able to communicate real life expectations to our mates or potential mates.

Loving on purpose in this way takes work. It takes drowning out what your momma taught you or what you watched. You have to be able to truly listen to yourself. Truly evaluate what will make you happy and stop comparing your life to others. There is no such thing as #relationshipgoals. Your goals should be getting in line with God's plan and purpose for your life individually which will lead you to the right partner.

When we base our relationship goals and expectations on others, we are setting ourselves up to fail. I distinctly remember reading a tweet with a person saying they just wanted a man to sing about them like John Legend sang to his wife in "All of Me." I processed it for a minute and then thought, "That will never happen." What he was singing about was unique to his experience. Sorry to break it to you but that cannot be recreated.

You may be thinking, "Ashley, it is really not that serious, this person was just talking about a nice song." And yes that could probably be the case and yes I do think way too much. But I do know that sometimes it's the simple things that we don't really think are that deep that can slowly drive a wedge in a good thing. Remember, when we focus on our love being intentional, deliberate and on purpose, that incorporates thinking of the little things.

It happens to the best of us, believe me. But each day, I learn to love on my own terms, my own way. I have plenty of couples that I think are great and that are positive influences in my life, but at the end of the day, this thing that I have is between me and him. And it should be that way. You and your partner against the world. You have to be very deliberate about what you let into your psyche and space making you think that what you have is subpar or less than. Be careful of coveting things that will never be your life. And don't go measuring up your partner to people they will never be. That goes both ways, with men and women.

Sometimes we really have to ask ourselves, "Am I the woman that I need to be for him to be the man I want him to be?" Or "Am I the man I need to be for her to be the woman I want her to be?" You may want your woman to let you lead, but do you have any idea where you are leading her? Are you following God's plan for both of you or are you making it up as you're going along and expecting her to go wherever you decide? Do you want him to be more involved with the children but undermine him at every chance that you get? Are you wanting him to submit to God but you're not spending any time with God yourself? This is big here and we have to be honest with ourselves.

We will look at other couples and think "I want that." But we are not half the woman or the man that it took to get that type of relationship. You cannot have what someone else "seemingly" has without putting in the work that it took to get there. And believe me, when you see people with great relationships, it took work! Get your expectations in line. Know what they are. Work on being able to communicate them to your partner and continue building on who you are in the process.

HeartCheck

Chapter Fourteen

- Are you holding others to higher standards than you hold yourself?

- Have you let outside sources influence your thoughts on your own relationship?

- What do you need from your relationship to make it most fulfilling?

....

"When we set the bar to impossible, all we will be met with is disappointment."

FIFTEEN
TRUE INTIMACY

Too often we only think of intimacy as sex. But honestly if that's all we see as intimacy, many of us have it wrong because so many don't even treat sex as an intimate experience. We're sharing it with anyone and everyone who winks at us and not really giving it the value it deserves. When I spoke as a part of the Urban Philadelphia Professionals Network (UPPN) mixer and conversation on love and relationships in Philadelphia, another form of intimacy was touched on – vulnerability.

Oddly enough, it's easier for many to just have sex with a person than to actually be able to be vulnerable with them. Kind of crazy at least in my little head. But vulnerability takes trust and we trust others more with our bodies than we do with our real feelings and authentic selves.

I touched on it a little on my blog before, but most of us tend to discard the trust that it takes to be vulnerable. As my Pastor says often many of us approach relationships with the "You ain't getting me," mentality. Our guards are way up. Most often based on not using a spirit of discernment at all when it came to previous relationships and so by the time we get to something authentic we have no idea how to receive it. Thus we have a bunch of guarded folks claiming to be in love with one another.

But I am here to tell you that if you have not learned to be vulnerable in your relationship, you have only really scratched the surface of the true connection that love brings. We think of vulnerability as a weakness instead of a strength. But it's easier to be guarded, that's why most people are. Our strength is in our ability, like the famous quote says, "to give someone the power to destroy our heart, but trusting them not to." That takes GUTS! That is a scary place to be for most of us.

So how do we get there? Well in any relationship, trust takes time to build. So you have to let it happen. The person on the opposite end has to prove that they are trustworthy with you inner most thoughts and feelings. You can't run around being a vulnerable mess with every person you encounter. It reminds me of our relationship with God, like I mentioned before on building trust. As new believers, we still have one eye open during prayer. It takes us time to really pour out our hearts and desires to God. But over time, he proves that he is worthy of our trust. Same with someone you are in relationship with. Get to know them. Spend a little more time listening than speaking all the time. What a person says and does will show you quickly whether they are someone you can really open up to. And if they're not, it may not be a good look to continue courting with that person. Trust is built of various parts. Does he come through when he says he will? Is she accountable for her actions? Does this person keep my inner most vulnerabilities protected or do they bring them up against me any chance they get?

In my own relationship, I know what scares him, I know what makes him uncomfortable, and I know what he is passionate about, his dreams, goals, and different desires of his heart. That is what truly will bind you to another person. We have to learn to get beyond the surface and superficial things that may have initially attracted us to that person. He trusts me enough with that. Even though at times I have screwed it up and shared too much with a friend or something like that, he still trusts me enough to say, "Hey don't share that with anyone." He's given me chances to get it right.

Sometimes we give others too many chances and sometimes we don't give people enough. There is a training process involved in love. We don't like to hear that. But we have to be trained in how to best love one another. Love is not one size fits all. Each relationship that we get involved with has a trial period where we have to learn what works and what doesn't for that particular relationship. We have to learn the inner workings of a person. What makes them comfortable, uncomfortable, happy, excited, and the list goes on. You can't skip this step. You can't be so worried about the physical that you aren't doing the work that it takes to really connect to the soul of another person.

Developing intimacy in your relationship is an ongoing process. The more that you experience together, the deeper the connection you create. Though we most often partner intimacy with the physical, it's a lot more than that. We experience various different types of intimacy in our relationships. This includes emotional connection, being able to share our innermost feelings with one another without judgment. We can connect spiritually with our partners, we connect around work, culture and a lot more.

Some of our most intimate moments as a couple have been routed in our spirituality. I can still remember this time before we were really officially dating when he asked me to pray with him. I think it was over the phone and I'm pretty sure I wasn't even saved yet. It threw me for a COMPLETE loop. Ha! I was looking at the phone like "what?" But that was really the start of something beautiful that I didn't realize at the time. It was the root of what would become such a strong point of connection in our relationship. Our faith. I felt awkward and confused, but we prayed. It was so weird for me, it was an unfamiliar place, but I was willing to trust him to lead me there. Willing to be a little vulnerable in that space.

We also have to learn to be sensitive to the challenges that our partners may face in the process of being able to be vulnerable. A lot of times we have walls and our loves ones do too affecting their ability to connect intimately with another person. So much of this is based on our earliest interactions with intimacy and growth in our families. Though all of us may not be naturals in the realm of intimacy, it is definitely something that can be developed and worked through.

Again, many of us are simply products of our upbringings and it can take some time to even realize it. For instance I grew up in a household where my mother wasn't this overly emotional person. She was loving, giving and a bunch of other great things, but she just wasn't so emotional. My dad on the other hand was a more sensitive person. A lot more like me. But I can really bounce between those different characteristics simply from being a product of that environment. But I have had to learn when I am being too sensitive and when I am being insensitive.

Don't be afraid to aide your partner in the process of learning how to be intimate with you in more ways than one. That's where communication comes in. You have to be able to tell your partner what you need from them in order to be more comfortable in those intimate spaces. Sometimes our partners are private, sometimes they need you to speak to them in a certain tone of voice, whatever it may be, be sensitive to those things if they have made it known to you. We don't come into relationships with all the answers. It's part of our role to help one another love each other the way that we want to be loved.

I've learned that the ability to be vulnerable is an act of faith. Vulnerability leaves us out there with seemingly no protection. But we have to have the faith that we will either be well received or that if we aren't, we will recover. Vulnerability has allowed me to lean into trusting God as my protector. There's that concept again. We constantly think that we have to protect ourselves and our feelings but if God be for us, who can be against us? (Rom. 8:31). God protects us physically on the daily basis, which we will most often buy into. We thank him that a car didn't rear end us or that we didn't fall down the steps or whatever the case may be. But I want to let you know that God can protect your heart too. Allow His strength to show through in your ability to be vulnerable.

We work so hard to avoid people actually seeing us. There may be some things that aren't so pretty inside that you have been working to keep hidden. With proximity comes disclosure. Your partner will see things about you and so you try to keep them at arms-length which really becomes impossible the longer you are with someone. When you are really in relationship with people, they will be all up in your world and it will not be easy to hide from them. I promise you that working through those things that you are afraid of exposing will be the only way that you can actually heal. Having an understanding of the person you are with or friends with or what have you, really can improve the relationship.

Think about someone who you may have met in your life and thought, "wow, why do they act like that?" Say someone who is always looking to be the center of attention. As you grow in relationship with that person, you may realize that they were dealing with feelings of neglect as a child and so they crave attention to help make them feel loved. Sure, they may still get on your nerves, but at least you now have a better understanding of why they are who they are. If you are actually in a relationship with that person, it may help you maneuver better instead of just getting so annoyed that they want your attention all the time.

These are real issues that present themselves in our daily interactions with one another. No, it's not about having someone all up in your business. It's about knowing how to explore who you are with the person you may be with in order to work past some hardships you may find in relating to one another based on your past experiences. When you love someone, you can't be afraid to show them your scars. Yes it takes time, but ultimately a wound that stays covered forever never properly heals. Eventually we all rip the bandage off to give it some air.

When this real bond is created with another person, the intimacy shared is deeper than sex. And cool, people like sex, but let me tell you, sex is easy, it's a dime a dozen and it's all over the place. It's easy to get and there is nothing impressive about that. True connection will help all the other areas of your relationship flow. True intimacy. That is when you know you have something real.

HeartCheck

Chapter Fifteen

- Have you ever been able to be truly vulnerable in a relationship?

- Have you only thought of intimacy as sex in the past?

- In what ways can you work to develop a deeper connection with friends, family, or your significant other?

....

"Vulnerability has allowed me to lean into trusting God as my protector."

SIXTEEN

WHAT SUPPORT LOOKS LIKE

Support is at the crux of the needs of both men and women. It seems to be instrumental in the decision to love another person. You are agreeing to be their support system in life, which has a lot of ups and downs that you have to be ready for. Truly supporting someone takes putting your own feelings aside at times to think about the best interest of another, which in a very selfish generation can prove to be difficult.

One of the scenarios ringing loudest in my head are careers. So many of us in this millennial generation are striving for lofty goals which take A LOT of time, planning, and hard WORK. When you are in a relationship, you have to be supportive of the goals and aspirations that your partner has. It's not just good enough to say "I support you." Real support is about being in the trenches. So if your girlfriend is trying to get her cake business off the ground there may be some nights you're helping her bake. Or if your boyfriend has a branding company, you may be attending networking events alongside him and aiding in market research.

Of course we all have our own aspirations, but I believe that when you really love someone, their aspirations become yours too. No, you don't have to give up anything that you're doing for your own personal fulfillment, but sometimes it takes some long nights or things you don't want to do to make certain that person feels like they have someone in their corner. The ability to make someone feel that way is in our actions and not just in what we say.

I often have mentioned that my now, husband is a music professional. Part of my support is knowing that sometimes his dreams take long nights at the studio and travel. In supporting him, I can't always complain about how late he's out or that he's been gone a long time on a working trip. Yes, I miss him and want that quality time with him, but the reality is, those are the sacrifices it takes for the things that he is reaching for. In that same way, there is not an event you won't see him attend of mine and he will get up early even after a long night at the studio to be right with me at my side, or to help me with whatever else I need. That is sacrifice, that is commitment, and that is real support.

A common theme in love is compromise and sacrifice like we've been talking about this whole time. I know that sounds scary and like something unfulfilling but it's very fulfilling when it's done right. As I mentioned in regard to compromising, when both people are giving, the results are masterful. You don't get 20 years in or 30 years in by being self-centered and "me, me, me" all the time. It is okay when you give of yourself in love, with a trustworthy partner. You will get so much in return. You would be shocked how much that person will try to meet your needs when they feel supported.

Stop tearing them down, stop complaining about their goals, and stop saying you support them and you never lift a finger to help them do anything. I learned this in hindsight really. In my life I have experienced people who in lip-service encouraged me to do things that I wanted to do, but they didn't want to jump in there with me. I didn't realize this was something that was lacking until I was out of the situation and able to see it from more of a 20,000 foot view. Your partner will not feel as supported if you are not truly invested in what it is that they're trying to do. Even outside of the goals that we are trying to achieve, our significant others go through difficult things with family, have their own personal challenges, feelings of being stuck and more. Be there to listen without always having your two cents, to give ideas when asked and most simply just to be a shoulder at times.

I've seen instances where someone is going through a hardship and though their significant other is supportive in the beginning, it's as if there is a time limit on it. We try to support, but don't realize just how ugly and just how dark it can get when things like a miscarriage or the death of a parent happens. Maybe someone loses their job or any of the other curveballs that life throws our way. In this instance is where we usually make a separation between being in a relationship and actually being married. "Well, I don't have to stick around if we're not married." You don't but is this the person that you see a future with? Is it long term? If so, I tend to believe that a married mind state begins well before we say I do. Are you marriage material?

When we talk about loving on purpose, things like support are at the crux of that notion. Loving someone when it's not easy or convenient or self-serving. That's the challenge. Being the one to encourage them when they don't want to get out of bed. Or helping them update their resume after the seventh failed interview. This is why I cannot simply reduce love to a feeling. There will be times when loving someone won't be pleasurable to our flesh, and may even hurt.

What keeps me encouraged is that I have seen couples come out of those dark places. I've seen them survive and in many cases come out stronger than before. We don't even really know the depth our character until it's tested. In that same way, it's hard to know if you even really know love when you've never been through anything. It takes time to see what you are really made of when it comes to this love thing.

Often, when we don't feel supported in our own relationship, this creates the perfect instance and opportunity to go looking for it elsewhere. Even if we are not actively pursuing it, sometimes an encouraging word or extra push from someone else can seem so appealing when we're starved of it at home. I always talk about being your mate's biggest cheerleader. No one should be cheering louder for them than you. And if they are, that's a problem. And if you notice, guess what, eventually they will notice too. This is where we see things like emotional infidelity take root, which leads to tons of other complications that really could have been avoided.

We all want to feel supported. But I will say for my ladies that this is really high on the "needs" list for men. I always liken it to how much women want to feel secure. Security helps us feel supported. Many women want to feel secure and many men want to feel supported. At the crux of all our antics and behaviors that's what most of us want. When we don't have that foundation, it tends to be detrimental to the connection that we have with our partners.

Let me say that there is never an excuse for stepping out of your relationship or marriage, but it is real life and something that I have seen tear people apart. I promised you real life in this book not any of the fairy tale stuff. Relationships don't thrive off cruise control. Every day that we wake up, we have to make a decision to put our best selves forward, to fight for what's ours, and to make our presence felt and revered in the life of our loved ones.

We all parade around like we are freestanding, independent and able to do it all. We pride ourselves on being on our own islands and self-sufficient. But there is nothing like the support of another person. It's incredible to have someone to help you to the finish line when you have no more left in you and someone who will be in your corner no matter what. Nothing worthwhile has ever remained upright without a supportive infrastructure intact. When there is no one left standing, you and your partner should be able to lean on one another. Again, not in a one sided way where one person is giving all of the support. When we are truly invested in another person, we invest in their dreams, their hardships, their struggles, their families and a whole lot more. If you are not ready for that type of investment, don't get into a relationship. Support is everything. It is part of the reason that God even created both man and woman. To be there for one another because two minds were way better than one. Give support and receive it.

HeartCheck

Chapter Sixteen

- Are you supporting your mate in theory and not in action?

- Has lack of support left you looking for it in other places?

- How can you step up to be more supportive in your relationships? What do you need from your mate in order to feel supported?

....

"Real support is about being in the trenches."

SEVENTEEN
LOVING ENOUGH TO LET GO

You may go through the chapters of this book and say, "Ashley, I have tried every part of this whole loving on purpose thing and it's still not working." Well, I have to be honest, you will find some moments in life where you have to be able to put yourself before all else and move on.

You won't ever catch me here trying to sell you a dream. I promise you that. At the end of the day, there are unfortunately times when you have to love someone enough to let them go. Think about God and His love for us. He could have easily decided to just dictate our whole lives but instead He gives us free will. And with that free will, sometimes we decide to completely stray away from His word. Like I did. There were times when I was completely disconnected from God. But he loves us enough to give us that choice. And guess what, He is right there waiting for us when we finally come to our senses.

I'm not suggesting that you wait for a person who has

clearly shown you that they are unfit to be in a loving relationship with you. But what I am saying is just because you have to let that person go, doesn't mean that you failed at loving them. Remember, we talked about the order of loving? God, yourself, and then others. Well, there will be times when you have to love God and yourself enough to expel toxic people from your presence. Really, anyone who is not supposed to be in your life won't be. But often we ignore a lot of the signs and we keep them around well past their welcome. Most likely experiencing a lot of pain and heartache that doesn't put us in great shape for the next person that may come into our lives.

Everything that we have talked about here works best when two people are willing to try. Unfortunately you cannot be in love by yourself. It just doesn't work that way. When you can trust that you have really given of yourself and it simply has fallen flat, then it's time to move on!

Sometimes I feel bad because I don't have as much sympathy as I should about the fourth or fifth time that someone has complained about the same exact behavior from the same person. Yes forgiveness, yes patience, but when we are talking unmarried and relentless, it may be time to move on.

> "When people show you who they are, believe them, the first time." – Dr. Maya Angelou.

So many of us make excuses for those that we love. It's almost an innate thing to try to do. But what happens when you are out of excuses? There is a decision that needs to be made about whether your mental and emotional well-being is more important than sustaining a relationship with that person. We complicate it a lot more than that. Yes sometimes we have children, and material things that get in the way. But I guarantee you, you will be better to your children mentally whole and at peace than trying to string together a relationship that's holding on by a thread.

We all make mistakes. We get things wrong. We get things wrong multiple times. But we have to learn to have a spirit of discernment to know when you may just be dealing with an inherent personality flaw. If that person cannot see it and is not working to correct it, you have to be able to pick up on that. For the most part, I believe that when you are in tune with the Holy Spirit, there is no way you would be comfortable staying in the presence of certain people. You would be at unrest, because you know they may not be a good person to have in your life. At the end of the day, you have to be on the same wavelength with another person and keeping God at the center alleviates a lot of confusion when it comes to relationships. I have learned this in my journey at least.

Real love does not easily dissipate. You will hear people say that love is not a choice and that you can't help who you love but I am here to tell you that you can certainly choose how you love them. Some people you need to love from afar. They don't love themselves enough to be in your presence and in your intimate company. You have to be able to recognize that.

It's really sad to see things fall apart in dating and especially in marriages. Don't be afraid to get help in those instances either from your spiritual counsel or a licensed therapist. I know that both parties aren't always willing, but if there is some hope there, take it. There is nothing like an objective point of view when you may be in turmoil in your marriage. It's even helpful to have that counsel before things get beyond repair. I was so enlightened during my premarital counseling. There were things that my Pastor was able to articulate to me about how my significant other was feeling that I never would have properly digested straight from him. There is no shame in getting help and often in certain communities we think that we can work out all our problems on our own.

We can't get caught up in the whirlwind of the wedding or what the church is saying about you being married. THINK, long and hard before saying I Do. Look at your expectations, think about your core values and really think is this someone I really want to go through thick and thin with? Make better decisions before entertaining the idea of marriage. And if you're past that, try everything you can before you ever utter the D word.

Take it to God instead of constantly nagging and yelling at your spouse. Sometimes if you can't get them right, He will surely convict them in the spirit. We also need to take it to him at times first instead of running to the phone to dish with girlfriends or guy friends that haven't had successful relationships in years. Pour your heart out to God, I am telling you that he is one of the BEST listeners and he is the one that can actually make the most change in your situation.

When we haven't yet made the commitment of marriage, then we have even more flexibility to decide what's for us and what may not be. Who we date and spend our time with matters if we are looking towards our future. If you're far off from that, then by all means, have fun and enjoy yourself in the process of finding a mate. But if you are farther along and really looking for something worthwhile, don't think that marriage or anything else is going to make a person change if they don't want to.

Don't jump from relationship to relationship without ever doing the inner work it takes to heal yourself and correct your bad habits. Honestly you will just take those problems right into the next relationship. I am saying that after you have exhausted all the options, tried to show someone that you are really in it and want to move forward with them and they are still giving you their behind to kiss, you have a choice to make. At the end of the day, you are responsible for your own emotional, spiritual and physical well-being. It is not the responsibility of the other person in your relationship. Should they behave better? Yes. But can you control their behavior? No. The one thing that you can control is you and your decision to be there.

We teach people how to treat us. So most often what is going on in your relationship is what you have allowed. I know that's a harsh pill for a lot of us to swallow, but it's a truth I have seen time and time again. But at any time, you can take a stand and decide that you are no longer going to let foul or unsavory behavior happen in your relationship. Then they will have a choice whether they will get their act together or whether they will pack their things and move on.

I still love people that I have not seen or heard from in years. If they needed anything I would do my best to help and I wish them all the best in their lives. But my love for you does not designate a space for you in my life.

There is truth to the saying that if you love something enough, let it go and it may return to you. And in the event that it doesn't it was never yours. I assure you that there is no such thing as a missed opportunity because what God has for you is undoubtedly for you. You may delay it by the choices you make and ignoring the Holy Spirit, but delayed doesn't mean denied like we so often hear.

Let go of your fear of what it will be like to be lonely or that you won't find anyone else. I heard Pastor Touré Roberts say, "alone does not have to mean lonely." Let go of the pride that will allow you to think that others' opinions of what happened in your relationship somehow matter. Let go of the unrealistic expectation that every person you meet is going to be "the one." Exercise your wisdom, seek God first, and all the things that you are looking for will be added. Remember, sometimes love may not come in the packaging you thought and sometimes it will be everything you need and nothing that you thought you wanted. But pray for the sensitivity to hear. And don't ignore it because you know when you know when it's right. You know when you know that this is the person, that years from now, even through the trials, even through the hard times, you can stand, alone, in the room when there is no one else.

And in that same vein, most of us know when it may be time to let someone we love go. It doesn't make you a bad person. It makes you an enlightened person who truly knows the importance of loving themselves enough to avoid negative people and situations. Above all else, guard your heart. Everything flows from it. (Proverbs 2:23).

HeartCheck

♦ What have you held onto long enough? It's time to go through it, so that you can allow yourself the space to experience something new.

♦ Have you done the inner work within yourself before jumping from relationship to relationship?

♦ In what ways do you need to begin putting things back in order? God, yourself, others.

....

"The one thing that you can control is you and your decision to be there."

EIGHTEEN

WHAT'S IN IT FOR ME?

I hope I have not belabored love for you. I know that it can feel like there is way too much sacrifice in love and you may be thinking, "What's in it for me?" I get it, believe me. Sometimes I wonder if my capacity to love is as big as my desire to. I want to be able to love people like God loves us. Although I know that I will never fully measure up, it's a goal to be actively seeking that type of love for my life. Have you heard the interpretation that we are God's love letters being read of men every day? It's so my hope that when people encounter me that they can see the influence of God in my life by the love that's radiating from me. Lofty goals, I know!

But I assure you, there is plenty in it for you. We tend to think that we constantly have to be out for ourselves in order to receive any fulfillment in life and that's not the case. God is our way maker. Our healer. Our comfort. Our provider. Our beginning, end, and everything in between. So why do we work so hard to do all these things for ourselves instead of leaning on Him which is really what He wants?

Most often we feel overwhelmed by the sacrifice involved in really loving others when we focus too much on ourselves. We think about everything that we are giving up and everything that we have to sacrifice. But we also have to remember that he who refreshes others will himself be refreshed. (Proverbs 11:25.) This is a principle that applies in many areas of our lives and especially in love.

When we love others, the way that they want to be loved. Not the way we think they should be loved or the way that we like to be loved which we project on them. But when we love others the way that *they* want to be loved, we have a much greater opportunity to in turn be loved the way we want to be as well. The biggest issue here is that most of us have learned a lot of selfish behaviors in love. We hold on to this childish idea of what love is supposed to be and we carry that into our adult relationships. When we have a solid foundation of what love truly encompasses, we realize that it was never about us in the first place.

God received nothing for giving of his Son. His love for us is the greatest love story ever told. God decided that while we were complete sinners, that He would send a savior to redeem us so that we could live life more abundantly. He thought of us first. Not what it would mean for Jesus, but what it would mean for the entire world. That's big. More than any of us would be willing to do for a loved one, let alone the whole world. And so here is this act, that changed the course of humanity that was rooted in love.

And it was difficult. I loved finding out that Jesus wasn't just willy nilly about going to the cross. He was afraid. He was sweating blood, but he was willing to stick to the assignment. He asked if there was ANY other way. But at the end of it, he realized, "Not my will, but your will be done." (Luke 22:42). He laid himself aside for the greater good.

The great thing about our love is that no one is asking us to physically go to the cross. If that was the case, none of us would be into this love thing. What I am asking, is that you crucify your old beliefs about love being self-serving. I'm asking that you crucify the pride and ego that is keeping you from truly being able to love to your capacity. These are much milder feats that we can surely conquer.

There will be stretching involved in the process. At times it will be really uncomfortable. At times you will want to give up and may say, "This is too hard, I just want to do things my way, I just want to quit." That is normal behavior. There are times when I am not sure that I can continually put myself aside and you know who is right there waiting in those moments? God, saying "You can do it." At this point in my life I almost feel like it is part of my mission to show people that we have a much greater capacity to love than we think. It's almost single-handedly what we were created to do. Above all these things, all these commandments, the greatest of all these is Love. (1 Corinthians 13:13.) You think that was by accident or something that God didn't really think was that important? NOPE! Or else He wouldn't have put that type emphasis on it.

When we decide to put love first, we will be able to keep every other commandment in perspective. We won't envy others. We won't steal or rob. We won't commit adultery. We won't do anything that degrades ourselves or others. Period. That's what love is all about. And I am here to encourage you that you can do it and on the other side of the stretching and discomfort, you will find something really beautiful. We focus way too much on what we're giving up as opposed to what we're gaining.

I think about my own relationships. There are times when I am frustrated, hurting, annoyed, defeated, lost, and all the other things that come along with loving people. But the moments when I am experiencing the fullness of love, far outweighs any of its challenges. It is truly, truly that powerful.

I may fuss, or fight, or be upset or whatever the case may be at times with my significant other. But the times when we laugh. I mean full hearted laughs that come from somewhere deep. Just the other day we laughed so hard together and I just closed my eyes and said thank you Lord. Thank you for giving me this amazing person to share these laughs.

Then there are the times when we catch each other's eye in a second of pure admiration. The real life moments where we have held one another up and been a true support to each other. The nights where there is no other place I'd rather be than right in his arms. The words of encouragement that are shared in times where I want to give up on myself, but he won't give up on me. There are some times when I look over at him and think, "how lucky am I to have someone to experience life with?" These are the most amazing moments I think you can experience in life. And it doesn't have to just be romantically. Think about the love that your children have for you which is undying. How privileged are you to have the opportunity to watch them grow and experience things for the first time? Think about the love that your parents have for you, even if they have made some mistakes. Think about the moments where friends stepped up and showed you that you were not in this life alone.

All of that is what's in it for us. Think about it. You have this life. You will try to accomplish things and amass material possessions and accolades and all that good stuff. But what will truly last? All of that will perish. We ourselves will perish. But LOVE will last forever. I don't care how many people are out here telling you that love is not important and to go get yours and chase the money and all that other foolishness. Love is what really matters. Not in this social currency way where if you haven't found a significant other you are somehow less than. I am talking about all types of love. There is nothing you can achieve that will be worth more than knowing what it is to be loved and knowing how to love someone other than yourself.

Each new generation is full of art, music and all types of creativity that often reflects all the intricacies of love. It's complex and simple all at the same time right? There is so much involved yet at the bare minimum it's what we're all longing for. Though sometimes we act out when we've been hurt and sometimes we are desperately trying to find our way, we need it. Love is as essential as the air that we breathe and when we are deprived of it, it can easily feel as if we are suffocating.

This is a chance to breathe new life into your relationships. Nothing and no one is ever perfect. It's one of the hardest things to really accept, though we really should know that. We aren't perfect and so how can we expect anyone else to be? But the imperfection of love seems to be what draws me to it. The mistakes, the low points, the redemption and the resilience is what's most impressive to me. If you're not impressed, I think you may be doing it wrong.

Loving someone, loving people, will sometimes take a lot out of you. But you are built for it. There is nothing that God has ordered us to do that he hasn't given us the capacity to do. So whether you are madly in love currently, desperately trying to find your way, or in need of rekindling some important relationships in your life, you can do it. Not in your own strength but in the strength that is perfected in your weakness. (2 Corinthians 12:9).

I will always believe in love and its power to completely transform the very fibers of our being. I know because God's love changed me. And each and every single day, I am thankful for that. It's like a veil was lifted from my eyes and I realized that I also had power. I wasn't a victim to my situation or to people or whatever the case may be. Deciding to love was my choice, a decision. I had to get intentional about what I was doing because I know what it's like to see love crumble and dissipate and there is no way that I wouldn't learn from those experiences.

We're so afraid of losing ourselves in relationships. I get it. We spend a lot more time being ourselves than learning how to adjust to moving on one accord with another person. Being in love and loving others doesn't have to change you, but I promise you it will challenge you. I believe that it will help you become the most refined version of who God has called you to be. God's love will mold you and your love for others will test you in what you've really learned. If you claim that you love God and cannot successfully love people, then you may want to assess where you are with Him.

In love you will grow. You will grow in ways that you may have never thought that you could have. In love you will experience an unexplainable joy and excitement. In love you will find beauty and worth and belonging. So much of purpose is birthed out of love and/or the lack there of which fuels us to find something bigger than ourselves to jump into. Love, my friend has a lot more to offer than you will ever be able to give or sacrifice. The ultimate sacrifice has already been made so your petty compromising and putting someone else first pales in comparison.

I am still growing in love, believe me. But I am in it. I am knee deep, making my way, and working to be completely enveloped in it. But it all starts with a choice. Will you choose to love on purpose?

HeartCheck

♦ Have you spent a lot more time focusing on what you would lose in a relationship as opposed to what you would gain?

♦ Are you always thinking "me first" when it comes to your relationships?

♦ Think about some of the best experiences that you have had with those that you love? Was it worth it?

....

"There is nothing that God has ordered us to do that he hasn't given us the capacity to do."

If you have really been feeling lost and afraid in love, I would love to pray with you.

Our Heavenly Father,
Lord I thank you for the opportunity to love on purpose. Lord thank you for being our greatest example of what it means to truly love. Lord allow us to walk in tandem with your designed purpose for us which was to put love before all else. Allow us to walk by faith and not by sight when it comes to love. Give us the wisdom and the discernment to know what is good for us and what we should stay away from. Lord manifest the fruit of the spirit within us. Aide us in our ability to hear from the Holy Spirit and to be living, breathing examples of your love. Your word says that perfect love drives out fear. Help us to kick the fear and to learn to give of ourselves wholeheartedly. Give us your strength to conquer our own apprehensions. Thank you for being our protector. Thank you for loving us first. In Jesus Name, Amen.

EPILOGUE

When we say that love is not a choice, we discredit all the hard decisions that we've talked about in this book that people in love make every day to stay in love. We are working against a lot. We work against a world that tells us that if you are unhappy, leave. Well, what constitutes unhappy and what happens during the times when you are not so happy but ultimately you have a good relationship? We work against a world that tells us that love is all about how it makes us feel. What happens when the feelings of lust and excitement change? Does the love go with it?

It's a lot to think about I know. But at the end of the day, I will always encourage you to exercise your power! You are not powerless in love. It is not a spell or something that takes over you. You are rooted in love. You are made in God's image and God is love. You were created to love, so it's always there. It doesn't magically come over you and magically you are in love. You have to choose. Every day you have to make decisions, but it gets easier.

We learn to put our pride aside. We learn to exercise patience. We learn the resilience of our hearts. We learn what it really means to put someone else's needs before our own. That is what real love requires. There are a lot of people in this love game without the credentials that it takes to make it work. Then we blame love or blame people and find ourselves bitter and jaded when really all the while, the only thing we could control in those situations were ourselves. Whether it was something we could have done in the relationship or whether we could have made a decision to love ourselves enough to walk away from a situation that was detrimental.

What I am saying is our love must be on purpose. It's not by happenstance or bad luck. It's not by way of artificial intelligence or the like. It's within every single one of us. We have the capacity to love boundlessly and we have the example in Jesus Christ of what that really and truly looks like. I promise you if you get a revelation of God's love for you, you will truly be able to grasp what love for one another should look like.

Perfect love drives out fear. (1 John 4:18). We can no longer be afraid to give of ourselves, afraid to let our guard down, afraid to say, "I want and need to be loved." We need it like air and water. It's what every human being on Earth is searching for. Whether it's in the bottom of a bottle or in the thrill of dangerous adventure, or the sheets of strangers – We are all trying to find it. Many of us are just looking in all of the wrong places.

I dare you to be intentional with your love. I dare you to make deliberate decisions. I dare you to choose and say, "I will love on purpose from this point on." You are not a victim to who you were or the lack of love you have received. You my friend, were made to love. Now go forth and prosper.

Dear Love Brunches

After writing my first book Dear Love: A Love Letter to You, I wanted to find a way to bring people together over great food to have great conversation so I created the Dear Love Brunch. I had no idea the bond and connection that would be created through these quarterly meet-ups. We talk, laugh, and there may even be a tear or two. I hope to bring a brunch to a city near you! If something of interest, I'd love to hear from you!

For more information:

www.writelaughdream.com

hello@writelaughdream.com

Made in the USA
Middletown, DE
24 January 2017